For Pearl Becker —

best wishes,

Judith Viorst

YES, MARRIED

YES, MARRIED

A Saga of Love and Complaint

JUDITH VIORST

Saturday Review Press
New York

Published simultaneously in Canada by
Doubleday Canada Ltd., Toronto.

Library of Congress Catalog Card Number: 72-79043

ISBN 0-8415-0207-2

Saturday Review Press
230 Park Avenue
New York, New York 10017

PRINTED IN THE UNITED STATES OF AMERICA

Design by Tere LoPrete

This book is dedicated, with love and thanks, to Sey Chassler and Silvia Koner, and to Ann Bray, Joanne Goldfarb, Polly Greenberg, and Barbara Rosenfeld.

Contents

❧❦❧

YES, MARRIED

I

Yes, Married

❧❦❧

I keep being told that marriage is on its way out, that I'm locked into an obsolete institution.

I keep being told that "till death us do part" is dead.

I keep being told, by unwed mothers and unwed lovers and communards and Women's Liberation, that the new life-styles will sweep away the old ones, that the mommy-daddy-kiddies family unit will shortly be replaced by—oh, wow!

Certainly the options these days seem wide open, and men and women are free now to combine in ways unheard of or, at least, not mentioned—when I was a girl.

Certainly, too, the Women's Liberation movement has altered both our awareness and expectations, so that it no longer appears to be written in the stars that to fellows come the tax-deductible lunches, and to us, the greasy frying pans.

And certainly the divorce statistics have something solemn to say about the lasting satisfactions of married life.

But yet, in 1971, flying in the face of the new-life-stylers, more than 4,000,000 Americans chose to get married. They clearly think it's still a good idea. And so do I.

The marriage that I write of in this book is populated by Milton, with whom I argue a lot, and by Anthony, ten, Nick, eight, and Alexander, four, on whose behalf I drive car pools, attend school plays, and wipe sticky grape or Kool-Aid off kitchen floors. It is also populated by me—hollering and crying, rushing and worrying, and in constant hopeless search of a perfect diet, a perfect sitter, a perfect vacation, and a perfect self.

The marriage that I write of in this book has nothing much to do with the lush, romantic visions of my youth. There are squirt guns, not fresh flowers, on my table. There are screams of "I'll tell Mom!", not strains of Bach. There is Diet Rite, not Beaujolais, at dinner. And the answer to "What's new?" is "The toilet seat broke."

The marriage that I write of in this book is almost 12 years old, and, as you'll see, I've rarely stopped complaining. But I think I know enough to love what I have, and to pray that it will endure till death us do part.

11

The Family That Fights
Together ... Fights
Together

❧⟨§⟩❧

I sometimes think of marriage as a series of shattered illusions, which start to shatter the day you walk down the aisle. The first one to go is the notion you've married your soul mate, a mirror image whose likes and dislikes, values, needs, and dreams are identical in every way with yours.

How, you may once have asked, could you fight with a soul mate?

Here's how.

Before my husband and I got married, we never had fights about anything. What was there, after all, to fight about? On every fundamental issue—war, peace, race relations, religion, education, Norman Mailer, the meaning of the universe—we were in total, sweet accord. Surely we had no reason to think that this mellow state of affairs would not continue for the next 40 or 50 years.

Oh, well . . .

From the minute we were married, we have managed to have fights about almost everything. What *isn't* there, after all, to fight about? Of course we're still in total, sweet accord on those fundamental issues—but so what? That still leaves us clothes, the telephone, cooking, driving, sex, money, in-laws, children, and who gets to read *The New York Times* first. And there isn't a prayer that this embattled state of affairs will not continue as we walk, hand in hand and still hollering, into the sunset of our lives.

I hadn't planned it that way. My marriage, as I all too frequently informed people in my premarital innocence, was going to be a mature, intelligent relationship. And if, perchance, some small disagreement happened to trouble the serenity of our days, it would be resolved promptly by rational discourse and fair-minded compromise. It was a swell plan. Unfortunately, it had nothing much to do with reality.

Reality, I found out in the course of our honeymoon, was my getting resentful about having to lend him my hairbrush and his getting resentful because I left the soap in the sink and not in the soap dish. Honestly, I didn't know until then that we even *had* positions on hairbrushes and soap dishes, but we do indeed. Furthermore, we also have positions on tucking in the blankets at the bottom and serving meals on paper plates and putting records back in their jackets and turning off the lights. We have, it turns out, passionately held positions on lots of dumb subjects, positions that we never dreamed we had, until we started living —day in and day out—with someone who failed to share our cherished views.

Although he now keeps his dandruff out of my nylon bristles and I try to keep the Ivory out of the sink, there is still plenty of fiercely uncompromised territory where warfare prevails.

• He thinks a comfortable house temperature is 68 degrees. I think a comfortable temperature is 84.

• He thinks a safe speed on the New Jersey Turnpike is 90 miles an hour. I think a safe speed is 45.

• He thinks it's unnecessary to enter checks in the checkbook. I think that not entering checks should be punishable by death in the electric chair.

• He thinks that when the rice is burning and Anthony has just dumped a dump truck on Alexander, I should get the hell off the phone. I think that when your best friend is pouring out her heart about what the painters did to her dining room, it would be inhuman to get off the phone.

Another big postmarital revelation was that husbands and wives expect all kinds of unexpected things from each other—things that were never mentioned back in those high-minded courtship discussions of loyalty, faith, trust, and undying devotion. Naturally we expected loyalty, faith, trust, and undying devotion. But did I know that he considered it a wife's solemn duty to fix fresh orange juice for breakfast and to pack his suitcase whenever he goes on trips? Did he know that I considered it a husband's solemn duty to keep the car filled with gasoline and to mail the letters? Of course not.

While both of us make an effort to live with our betrayed expectations, there are times when I am moved to phone him in the middle of an important business meeting just to mention that the tank is empty and the letters are still sitting on the mantel, and he says he'll call me back later, and I say maybe there won't *be* any later, and he reminds me that he hasn't had a glass of fresh orange juice for more than 11 years, and I tell him to get a valet if he wants someone to do his packing for him.

Unless one of us has hung up by then, we go on to review every unfulfilled expectation of our married life. How could a wife run off to have her hair done when her husband is lying at home in bed with a possibly terminal sore throat? How could a husband not drive a wife downtown when she was four months pregnant? How could a wife forget, year after year, that a husband likes unsalted butter? How could a husband forget, year after year, that a wife likes her martinis on the rocks? How could a wife display an almost deliberate failure to grasp what kinds of ties would make a husband happy? How could a husband buy a wife a size 16 skirt when any stranger can see she is almost a 12?

My third discovery was that even though a husband and wife may love each other more than anyone in the world, they can also be ruder and rattier to each other than to anyone in the world. Where else, I ask you, but in the warm intimacy of marriage does a woman tell a man that only a pretentious idiot could have enjoyed that movie? Where else but in the tender security of marriage does a man tell a woman that she looks like an overweight gym teacher in that jump suit?

I know it shouldn't be that way, but it is. Somehow marriage makes it possible for me to ask my husband (after he has repaired the bicycle and plastered the hole in the front hall and played touch football with the kids), "So how come you didn't remember to take out the garbage?" Somehow marriage makes it possible for my husband to ask me (after I have served him clams casino and rice with fresh mushrooms and asparagus vinaigrette), "So how come we always have jello for dessert?"

Given a certain number of uncompromisable convictions and a certain number of unfulfilled expectations and the fact that marriage evokes in people not only their best but also their beastliest features, any couple is bound to have their fair share of fighting. If in addition they are not especially obliging or unduly cheerful or strenuously opposed to controversy (all of which I am not), fighting may become a basic feature of married life.

I should say right now that I'm certainly not suggesting that all marital battles are frivolous. There is nothing frivolous about some of the fights that are fought when he wants cognac followed by a night of love and she wants a hot bath followed by a night of sleep, or when he thinks his mother should visit for a week and she thinks his mother should visit for 15 minutes, or when he feels she'll never understand him and she feels he'll never understand her either. But marriage also seems to be the setting for vast numbers of dumb and essentially nonessential battles that occur because soap-dish disagreements and orange-juice disappointments are escalated to civil war.

In our household escalation often happens when it's too early in the morning or too late at night. Take 7:15 A.M., when, according to my youthful dreams, my husband and I were going to awake full of love and cheer, and immediately launch into a vivacious discussion of existentialism. Instead, I am groping my way out of bed feeling crabby and put-upon while he is coldly informing me that there isn't a single pair of matching socks in his drawer.

Now theoretically it might be possible to respond with gracious good humor to this vicious attack on my role as wife, mother, and sex partner. Theoretically it might even be possible to see his remark as something other than a vicious attack. But 7:15 A.M. is not one of my finer moments —and it definitely is no time to talk to me about socks. So I point out to him that just because his parents catered to all his infantile needs doesn't mean that I have to perpetuate this kind of crippling emotional dependency. The morning deteriorates from there.

Escalation from border skirmish to total war also occurs whenever one of us is under pressure and overwrought.

Since he is the calmer grown-up in our family, he is rarely in this state except when his work is going badly, or when he is making out our tax returns, or when, in the course of my tidying up his desk, certain crucial documents vanish forever.

I, on the other hand, can go into a spin if the car breaks down or Alexander throws up or a colony of ants invades the kitchen. It's easy for us to fight then, because I can frequently devise a way of blaming my husband for my sufferings (even if he's in Chicago at the time, in which case we have an expensive, long-distance fight) or because he may be foolhardy enough to blame me. "I told you that those kids eat too much junk," he says. "I told you ten days ago to spray the kitchen," he says. What kind of woman would take that lying down?

I'm probably at my most overwrought, however, when we entertain. For reasons that doubtless have to do with my early toilet training, the prospect of six couples coming at 8:30 transforms me into a four-star general conducting a major campaign. All by myself I can convert a happy home into a battlefield. It goes like this:

At ten o'clock I can be found slaving over the stove, surrounded by flour and butter and cookbooks, and responding to the friendliest questions with a tight-lipped "Leave me alone. Can't you see I'm in the middle of the béchamel sauce?"

At lunch I announce that anyone who drops one solitary cracker crumb on my freshly vacuumed rug—daddies included—will get no dessert until 1979.

At four o'clock I pick up the Saturday paper, which my husband has callously dropped on the coffee table next to my exquisite flower arrangement, and demand in a tear-choked voice, "Are you trying to ruin everything?"

At five Nicky comes in with a cut on his chin and I

shriek, "Don't bleed on the couch, for God's sake! Go in the bathroom and bleed!"

At 6:15 I notify my husband with narrowed eyes that now, right now, is the only possible time for him to shave and take his shower.

At 7:15 I notify the children, in tones that would strike terror into the heart of Moshe Dayan, that they have precisely one hour and 14 minutes to put on their pajamas, wash, get into bed, and fall instantly to sleep.

By the time the doorbell rings Milton has suggested that I am a fascist, an unfit mother, and mentally unbalanced, and I have suggested that he is a sadist, an unfit husband, and morally rotten. Smiling between clenched teeth, we greet our first guests.

Even when we're neither tired nor harried, we can transform dumb disagreements into ferocious fights if we're particularly unhappy with ourselves and feeling unloved or if we're particularly pleased with ourselves and feeling unappreciated.

I remember one afternoon, for instance, when I had taken the three kids, and their two cousins besides, to go bowling, which can make for quite a messy afternoon. Also, it was snowing, and there had been all those mittens and boots, and while we were driving home I got a flat, and . . . Anyway, I had coped magnificently. By the time I walked into the house I was at least Joan of Arc, and would not have considered a flourish of trumpets inappropriate. Instead, my husband looked up wearily from the sofa (where he had been watching the football game all day) and asked me would I please go get him a Schlitz. I would rather not divulge my response to his question.

After several years of fighting, Milton and I are quite familiar with how, when, and why many of our battles begin. We are quite aware that, given the right circum-

(11)

stances, an admiring comment withheld, a failure to display appropriate sympathy, a little unsolicited advice, a bit of criticism, or the most innocent reference to another's achievements or charms can lead us straight over the cliff. We have both learned that it is unwise for me to ask provocative questions like "What would you do if Myrna begged you to sleep with her?" or "Who is the most intelligent woman you ever met?"—and even unwiser for him to give me an answer.

He knows very well that when he hangs around the kitchen making helpful little culinary observations like "You need more oregano in the marinade," he is asking for trouble. And I know very well that when he forgets his glasses and I offer little psychological observations like "You had an unconscious desire not to see this movie," I am asking for trouble too.

What with all this wisdom and knowledge and understanding, we can now launch a first-class fight whenever we choose. Once begun, it doesn't really matter whether the initial issue was dripping on a newly waxed floor or drooling over a newly divorced blonde; the tone and style of our fights are always pretty much the same.

He starts out cool and scornful, sometimes even disdaining to reply to what he terms my "berserk distortions of fact." (In his opinion I do a great deal of berserk distorting.) I, as might be expected, am considerably hotter and louder. There is an exchange of accusation and counteraccusation, followed by denunciation and counterdenunciation, all of which is accompanied by citations of past and potential grievances.

At some point he makes an effort to disengage himself from the battle by retreating into a newspaper or even by leaving the room. He never succeeds. I scream. I follow. I call him names that nice wives shouldn't know. And I manage to goad him, sooner or later, into being as noisy and irrational as I.

On two or three occasions, in fact, I have even inspired him to raise a threatening hand in my direction. And once I actually managed to parlay a modest poke into assault and battery by falling to the floor, rolling over a few times, and announcing, for the ears of our thunderstruck baby-sitter, "I am sick and tired of all these brutal beatings."

I would like to say that we're at least discreet enough never to fight in front of our friends or our children. I would like to say it—but it isn't true. Given sufficient provocation we have tangled at cocktail parties, dinner parties, the swim club, and peace marches. Our children have heard us holler plenty, too, but I suspect it doesn't hurt them to learn that we're allowed to be angry even with people we love.

Among the fighting couples we know—and we do know quite a few—we are noted for a certain lack of restraint. Other husbands and wives conduct entire battles in whispered snarls or with oblique digs or by relying heavily on punishing silences. I even know one lady whose ice-blooded husband holds up his end of their fights with written replies, which usually begin, "Nuclear to our disagreement of the twelfth . . ."

I've tried out most of these sophisticated techniques, but I find that they're simply not my style. My whispered snarls disintegrate into roars, my oblique digs into direct blasts, and the only person I punish when I'm silent is myself. As for the written reply, I haven't yet attempted it, but I'm afraid that if I did I would wind up hitting my husband on the head with the typewriter.

Despite all the tumult and shouting, however, our marriage survives our battles very well. It survives because we never, even in our wildest exchanges, say anything that we can't, in our saner moments, laugh about. And it survives because we never fail to make up.

Making up in our household is rarely a formal affair. I know that some couples insist on ritualistic apologies, which may range from total recantation to "I'm not taking back what I said, but I'm sorry for the way I said it." I know others who actually sit down at some point and negotiate a settlement. But these methods have rarely succeeded with us. If Milton apologizes, I decide he should take back everything he has ever done in our entire marriage. If I apologize, he decides he doesn't like the tone in which I'm saying I'm sorry for what I said. And forget about those negotiated settlements—they have had an unfortunate tendency, whenever we've attempted them, to lead to an immediate resumption of hostilities.

So what we do instead, when one of us is battle-worn and longing to be friends, is simply to announce, "I won't be mad if you won't"—and it's over. I'll admit that this doesn't resolve the initial disagreement, but then, we often can't remember what that was.

On countless occasions, in the after-fight afterglow, we both have made the most beautiful resolutions.

I won't complain anymore when he's not on time.

He won't complain anymore if I use his razor.

I won't tell him he just went through a stop sign.

He won't tell me I just ruined the scrambled eggs.

For a full 24 hours we walk around the house suffused with the noblest feelings of tolerance and generosity, convinced that we will never fight again. We agree, do we not, on the fundamental issues? What is there, after all, to fight about?

It was during one of these after-fight afterglows that Milton and I decided to buy a house. It sounded like a swell idea at the time, but it turned out to open a whole new field of battle.

The cause of our conflict wasn't which house to buy. The house, oddly enough, we quickly agreed on. Our hostilities stemmed, instead, from the fact that a full four months before our moving date, I started making preparations to move.

Throughout this difficult period in my life, Milton kept saying unhelpful things like "Relax." He said that if we accepted the fact that we were embarked upon an ugly and harrowing experience during which we would scream at each other, loathe each other, and maybe even attempt to destroy each other, it wouldn't be so ugly and harrowing.

He also said that if I ever again pulled anything like packing up the Bufferin and his toothbrush a full four months before our moving date, he would destroy me.

Furthermore, Milton took the troublesome position that the secret of successful moving was not in the Packing Up but the Weeding Out. That's one of those positions which, I'm afraid, is only sound in theory.

For from the moment that he latched onto this notion, we fought, with increasing bitterness in our hearts, about exactly what would be packed and what would be weeded.

Milton, for instance, refused to give up his silk shantung trousers, made for him during the Korean War by an apprentice Hong Kong tailor who was surely in the pay of the enemy. Although I tried explaining to him that these trousers were, by any objective standards, not only unwearable but an affront to art, to nature, and to the human body, he would not yield.

And yet this very same person who wouldn't weed out his trousers expected me to divest myself of all the precious letters I had saved, with great devotion, over the years. These were letters, mind you, from my friend Phyllis, asking about my strep throat; from the Heart Fund, thanking me for collecting on the block; and from the preschool, naming me Alternate Non-Voting Board Member in charge of crayons.

To a sensitive human being, as I told Milton, these letters —when taken together—revealed the odyssey of a life. Milton replied that he wasn't, thank God, that sensitive.

But it wasn't just trousers and letters we couldn't weed out, or his baseball mitt that won the game in high school, or my 14 jars of beauty cream that failed. Between the two of us, we had developed emotional ties to every unreadable book, every empty jelly glass, every obsolete medication, every chipped ashtray in our house.

One week, to give you an example, I tried to dispose of a half-used tube of diaper-rash ointment on the grounds that (a) our youngest hasn't worn diapers in more than two years, and (b) we'd retired from reproduction. I won't explain why Milton thought we should keep it, except to say that it concerned certain Acts of God.

What made these disagreements so painful, I'm afraid, were the aspersions we cast on each other's values and dreams.

A man who wants to cling to Korean War pants, I told him, is more than a militarist. He is a man harboring secret longings to return to his youth and to evade his familial responsibilities.

Milton was equally invidious about my beauty creams. "Why," he inquired cruelly as I wrapped the Ardens and Rubinsteins, "don't you give up?"

As I saw it, I was trying to be this wonderfully organized person and Milton was trying to thwart me. For even when we both agreed to *not* weed something out, he wouldn't let me pack it.

One Wednesday, for instance, I packed away our heating pad, which none of us had used in seven years.

That Thursday Milton developed lower back pain and needed dry heat.

On Friday I put the waffle iron—we'd never once eaten waffles in our house—into a carton.

On Saturday morning, guess what he craved for breakfast?

Milton said we must try to remember, through this ordeal of moving, our love for each other. I said we must try to remember, through this ordeal of moving, that the cartons had to be filled when the movers arrived.

We almost didn't.

You should not think for a moment that our moving battles ended when we moved. For the miseries of moving are divided into two miserable parts—the Getting Out (of the old house) and the Getting In (to the new).

As I think I've already made clear, the Getting Out part was nasty and vicious and mean. Fortunately we were saved by the fact that one beautiful day, as we stood around hurling insults at each other, the moving men arrived and carried our couch through our old front door and into a van. We had, willy-nilly, Gotten Out!

All that was left, then, was to carry this couch through our new front door and into our new living room and place it . . . and place it . . . where?

Ah, that is the question we've been trying to answer, along with lots of others, for several months now. For the Getting In part of our moving isn't yet over—and maybe it never will be.

Why is this so? Am I inefficient? Am I disorganized? Do I have trouble making up my mind? Certainly not. Our household is a mess for one simple reason—my husband.

For Milton is a man who has something to say, not only about busing and the FBI and the state of the economy, but also about where the living-room couch should go. And what fabric it should be reupholstered in. And what color that fabric should be. And whether, to complement the couch, we need one large coffee table to set in front of it, or two small side tables to flank it. And so on.

THE MAN IS DRIVING ME INSANE!

You realize, I suppose, that all over America women are complaining that their husbands don't give a damn about such matters. "He never notices anything," they sigh. "If only he'd take an interest in the house."

These are obviously women who don't know what well off is, and how lucky they are to be married to the kind of fellow who, even if it were a question of life or death, couldn't tell you if his kitchen were yellow or green. The color of *our* kitchen, let me just add, is still white, because Milton thinks the green I want is vulgar and I think the yellow he wants is wishy-washy.

I suppose, in all fairness, I should also mention that many of our Getting In disagreements have to do with the crude subject of money, about which my husband is rather more realistic than I. He seems to feel quite strongly, for instance, that putting our furnace into working condition takes precedence over the purchase of four gilt cherubs which would look adorable hanging by long golden chains from our dining-room ceiling.

Nevertheless, what he said about those cherubs was very impolite.

But then, politeness is not a significant feature of our marriage at the moment, as everyone on our new block undoubtedly knows. Our disagreements, vigorously expressed, have already given our neighbors quite an earful. And if we don't, very soon, decide whether our bedroom windows will have shades, shutters, drapes, or Venetian blinds, I'm afraid we'll be giving them quite an eyeful too.

In fact, I can see it now—we'll become a scandal. The Neighborhood Association will ask us to leave. And I think I'd do anything, sacrifice anything, never to move again.

I might even stop fighting with Milton.

III

How Did I Wind Up
with Boys?

❧❧❧

Our kids, like our fights, seem to have been with us always.
It's sometimes hard to recall when I *wasn't* a mom.

Or a mommy.

Or a ma.

Or, in less blissful moments, You Mean Old Thing.

What I've also often been, since I've been a mother, is inadequate to the task—outflanked, outnumbered, and out-
run. This isn't because there are three of them and only one
of me. It's because—forgive me, feminists—they're boys.

For I am, you see, a neat and cautious lady. In my closets
all the hangers face the same way. I am pained by the sound
of loud voices, the sight of fresh blood. My athletic skills
can be summarized in five words—I float on my back. Dirt

and disorder distress me; God never intended me to go on a camping trip; and the spectacle of a small child trying to leap from the top of a 12-step stairway makes me sick to my stomach.

I was clearly meant to be the mother of girls: of quiet, orderly, gentle little girls; of dainty, well-mannered, un-grubby little girls for whom I could buy dear velvet dresses with lace collars and dolls with curly hair.

I was clearly meant to be the mother of girls. So how—Lord help us all—did I ever wind up with three sloppy, wriggly, blood-dripping, baseball-playing, loud-mouthed, fresh, and fierce little boys?

Wait, I know what you're thinking. And I won't dis-agree. Yes, I'm sure you can show me girls who are fierce and noisy, and lots of gentle little boys as well. But we needn't get into that discussion now. For I only want to ex-plain what it's like in *our* family, what it's like for a let's-cut-out-paper-dolls, let's-put-polish-on-our-nails kind of mother to be raising these let's-climb-out-on-that-tree-branch-and-see-if-it-will-break kind of sons.

As a matter of fact, I think I'll start with that tree branch, or at any rate with those perilous activities that my boys somehow always find so tantalizing. For it has been my heart-attack-making experience to observe that if there's thin ice to skate on, my sons will go and skate on it; and that if there's a hole big enough to get their heads *into* but not *out of*, they'll go stick their heads in it; and that if there's a deadly drop between the Tuttles' roof and the Biermans' roof, they won't be content till they've jumped from one to the other.

I don't understand it. But then, I've never understood mountain climbing, or shark hunting, or automobile racing, or swimming the English Channel. Why, as I say to my boys, ask for trouble? But their reply to this piteous cry is cruelly simple: ask-

(*21*)

ing for trouble is fun. And let me tell you, there's no way to stop them from asking.

This past summer, for instance, I took my four-year-old to Kiddie Land, and carefully chose for him only the safest rides. It was bad enough, I thought, when—mid-spin on the merry-go-round—he switched from the black horse to the white horse, in the course of which he caught his foot in the stirrup and finished the ride upside down.

But at least the merry-go-round was on the ground.

The fighter-pilot ride, on the other hand, whirled high above my head, and as soon as Alexander was sure I couldn't intervene, he unhooked his seat belt and—Oh, no! My God! I can't bear it!—crawled out of the gun turret and onto the wing of the plane.

"Why, why, why?" I screamed, when he returned, un-smashed, to earth, and I was smacking and hugging him simultaneously. "Why do you have to do such crazy things? Why can't you get on the rides and just plain ride them?"

Alexander had an answer to that question. "I just plain rode them last year," he explained. "This year I wanted to ride them fancy."

Well, I asked myself, what else did you expect from a kid who spent his infancy poking metal keys into electrical outlets and having his stomach pumped at the Poison Clinic?

Ah yes, the Poison Clinic. And the waiting room at Dr. Ross's office. And the emergency room at George Washington Hospital, to which I rush the crushed fingers, the twisted ankles, the chipped bones, the mashed noses, and the skull fractures—with one intern patching up my wounded son, and another giving smelling salts to me.

"I think you ought to step outside, ma'am," a doctor once told me, watching me pale as he took 14 stitches in Nick.

"Don't be silly, I'm fine, I'm really fine," I replied. And

then, to prove how fine I really was, I tossed my smelling salts into the waste basket—and passed out cold.

Nick, I might mention, was recently informed by the school nurse that while he had only the *second* highest number of accidents of any child in grades kindergarten through eighth, he was number one as far as *major* accidents were concerned.

He was very proud.

And I am very wrung out. On the week Nick collected three concussions in six days, I burst into tears and said to Dr. Ross, "What shall I do? How will that kid survive his childhood? How will *I* survive his childhood?"

Dr. Ross patted me on the arm. "Mrs. Viorst," he said, "when you have sons, you've got to figure that several times a month you'll be filled with terror."

And I am, I am. While my friends with girls buy their Band-Aids by the box, I buy them by the case. And while their daughters may display a scratch or two, my sons are already scarred for life.

I'll willingly concede that somewhere there are boys who have no interest whatsoever in finding out what will happen if they walk backwards down an up escalator. But these boys, alas, are not mine. I'll even concede that somewhere there is a mother who, when her son *does* walk backwards down an up escalator, will not get chest pains, shortness of breath, and a pounding headache. But that mother, alas, is not me.

For I was clearly meant to be the mother of girls. We could look through the rings in my jewelry box together, and I could teach them how to make pretty paper fans. They wouldn't prefer to split their lips riding bikes—eyes closed and no hands—down very steep hills. They wouldn't tell me I had to play in the outfield. They wouldn't say, "Let's race," and even if they did, maybe they wouldn't beat me all the time.

(23)

What makes it so hard, you see, about raising boys isn't only the risks they take, and the accidents they have, and the blood they shed. It's also their exhausting *physicalness*.

At the moment, for instance, I'm the only one in our family without a baseball mitt. And I'm afraid they plan to buy me one for my birthday. I'm also afraid they would gladly trade me in for two pitchers, one fullback, or a Harlem Globetrotter. And why not? What good, after all, is a mother who won't go camping or hiking (suppose we meet snakes?), who never gets any basketballs in the basket (who can *see* that far?), and who cries whenever they tackle her in football?

A daughter wouldn't *want* to tackle me—or twist my arm until I hollered uncle. Nor would she feel particularly pressed to resolve all those who-gets-the-last-piece-of-gum disputes by means of physical violence.

"Why don't you guys sit down and talk it over?" I ventured one day, when Anthony and his best friend, Tommy, were thrashing about on the floor, swapping blows.

Anthony dodged a fist and looked up at me. "But, Mom," he replied, "we *are* talking it over."

My boys do lots of talking with their bodies. And they don't seem able to keep their bodies still. It is, for instance, beyond their human capabilities to sit quietly in a chair for 60 seconds straight without wriggling, writhing, and eventually falling out of it.

Now girls—the ones that I know, anyway—don't seem to be as . . . twitchy . . . as most boys. My good friend Irwin once told me that a single sheet of paper could keep his daughter occupied for hours.

"She'd color it, she'd fold it, she'd cut it, she'd paste it," he said, "and then, after that, she'd kiss it and hug it and pat it."

I, on the other hand, know exactly what would happen if I gave that same sheet of paper to one of my sons. He'd either rip it to shreds or swallow it—immediately—and then he'd say, "There's nothing for me to do."

How in the world did I ever wind up with boys? They bleed, they play baseball, they fight, they twitch—and they're fiercely competitive. Oh, my girl friends' daughters are quite competitive too, but it seems to me that they do it far more gracefully.

"Her dress is very pretty," I heard an Ellen observe the other day. "But my dress is very prettier."

My sons would never phrase it like that—never. When they compete, they make no bones about it. "Mine's great," is what they'd say, "and yours stinks."

They wouldn't say it softly and sweetly, either. Softly and sweetly is not how my sons speak. Their *whispers* at the supermarket—"Hey, Mom, I've gotta go. I've gotta go bad"—can be heard six aisles away. And when they talk in what they conceive to be normal tones, their voices can be heard outside in the parking lot, even if—as my husband recently established—you get in the car, close all the windows, and turn on the radio.

I've often tried explaining to my boys that it really isn't necessary to convey the simplest little messages in ear-splitting bellows and roars. But bellowers and roarers is what they are. And thumpers and thudders and bangers and slammers, too, as if it is their personal mission in life to stamp out silence.

They're very good at it.

A few weeks ago, for instance, the whole family went to eat hamburgers in a rather rough part of town. Our restaurant, in fact, was patrolled by a private policeman, whose job it was to get rid of the rowdies and drunks. During the brief period that we were in there, this policeman was called upon three separate times to threaten to throw out certain disruptive elements.

All those disruptive elements were mine.

I also remember the day we went to the shoe store and my sons decided to entertain the customers by singing those awful songs that little boys learn in the little boys' room at school. In their exuberance, unfortunately, they stumbled over a couple of standing ashtrays, one of which toppled into—and wiped out—an elaborate display of imported Italian sandals.

At that point our pale and harried salesman turned us over to a younger, stronger salesman, muttering under his breath, "Take them. They're yours. It isn't worth the commission."

I had no grounds on which to be insulted.

But please don't think for a minute that I'm merely smiling benignly through this madness. I am not. I am seizing my boys by their collars. I am bopping them on their behinds. I am thrusting them into their chairs and swearing that they will suffer horrible punishment if they don't CUT IT OUT IMMEDIATELY.

They stare back at me with hurt, bewildered eyes. "Cut *what* out?" they want to know. "We were just being friendly."

How did I wind up with boys? They're twitchy. They're competitive. They're loud-mouthed. They're public nuisances. And they're private nuisances, too, incapable of walking from one end of the living room to the other without inflicting permanent damage upon it by spilling something, or knocking down something, or denting the marble-topped coffee table with something.

Why, I've often wondered, should this be?

Sometimes I think they're clumsier than girls. Sometimes I think that maybe they're just more careless. And sometimes I think boys were born with pointier elbows, and slipperier fingers, and an urgent and fundamental drive to wipe their gooey, slimy, sticky hands on the curtains, on the walls, on their clothes, on *my* clothes—on anything as long as it isn't a napkin.

Which leads me to another observation—my sons are slobs. In their philosophy, neatness doesn't count. They are handsome fellows, honestly they are, but the sight of them in their smeary, mismatched outfits is enough, I swear, to make a hippie wince.

And enough to break the heart of a clothes-loving mother, of a mother who likes the blues to blend just right, of a mother who—whenever she goes to the boys' department—always makes a stop at the girls' department to gaze longingly at the ruffles and ribbons and lace.

But then, resigned and thwarted, I walk on—in search of clothes that possess, not charm or beauty, not appliqués or butterflies or bows, but . . . stamina.

Why do I bother? With boys like mine, their clothes don't stand a chance. Whatever it is I select, they'll jam the zippers. And they'll pop the buttons. And the seams will unravel and gaping holes will appear. Their *pockets*, for heaven's sake, will start falling off, and every other remaining accessible surface will be covered by the kinds of wrinkles and stains for which modern science has yet to find a cure.

"*That's* how you let the children go to the movies?" my in-laws, down from New Jersey, asked me last spring.

And much as I'd have loved to contradict them, it wasn't possible.

For there was Alexander, in a shrunken shirt with smudged black horizontal stripes ("But, Mommy, that's not dirt. That's just spaghetti") and shrunken trousers with smudged red vertical stripes ("But, Mommy, that's not dirt. That's Coca-Cola"), and two entirely unrelated socks.

And there was Nick, in a pair of baggy shorts that sank down to his ankles whenever he inhaled ("I do too know where all my belts are. One is at school, one is at David's, and one we cut up to make headbands") and a formerly orange top that was surely the rottenest tie-dye job in town.

And there was Anthony, in a pair of jeans whose patches' patches had patches ("Grandma gave me a dollar to throw them away. I gave it back") and a faded purple polo shirt with a stretched-out neckline large enough to accommodate the head of an elephant.

And believe me, if I'd told them to go in and change, they'd have returned with something even more revolting. For although I always buy them nice little outfits like green plaid trousers with matching pale green top, or navy trousers with matching red-and-blue-striped shirt, they always wind up wearing the green plaid trousers with the red-and-blue-striped shirt.

How, I would like to repeat, did I wind up with boys? They don't want to be the best-dressed kid on the block. "You look darling," I once said to Nick, when—after a fight to the finish—he was bludgeoned into white ducks and a gold-buttoned blazer. Nick clutched at his stomach and made horrid gagging sounds. "Who," he groaned in disgust, "wants to look *darling!*"

No, I can't say words like *darling* to my boys. They do not like their mother talking mushy. Nor is it ever possible, these days, to get them talking mushily to me.

"A penny for your thoughts," I'll sometimes offer, hoping they'll say how much they love their ma.

"Yesterday we cut a worm in half," Anthony will reply, "and Iggie Halpern ate it."

Other cozy conversations with my sons have revealed their views on Rice Krinkles and baseball cards and nose bleeds and picking scabs. Or maybe they'll ask me some deep philosophical question, like "Would you rather choke to death or burn to death in a fire?" Or, if they're feeling terribly intimate, they might confide that Joel down the block has smelly feet.

I'm sure it wouldn't be that way with a girl. We'd cuddle up to each other, full of endearments, and she'd tell me why Marjorie wasn't her very best friend, and then we'd discuss whether braids were better than ponytails, and then if I happened to give her a kiss or two, she wouldn't spend several minutes rubbing her cheek as if she'd been fatally contaminated.

I'd fully intended to be the mother of girls.

But, as you see, it didn't work out as I'd planned.

So I live in a completely masculine household, where everyone showers together except for me, where the seat of the toilet is always lifted up.

And I use lots of Band-Aids. And I play in the outfield. And I steal whatever kisses that I can.

And someday, I comfort myself, they'll learn to speak softly. And they'll learn to sit quietly. And they'll stop having fights, and their tops and their bottoms will match. There will be no more stains on the carpet, no dents in the tables, no naughty songs that they learned in the boys' room at school.

There will be no more shrieks of "Mommy, come quickly, I need you."

And God, how I'll miss it. How I will miss it all.

IV

Who's Minding the Kids?

❧❦❧

While I'm sure I'll shed a tear when the kids are grown, what I don't expect to miss are their baby-sitters.

Trying to find one.

Trying to find one I like.

Trying to find one the kids like.

Trying to find one who's able to stand the kids.

Trying to find one under whose care my boys will still be intact when I return home.

Trying to . . .

My four-year-old is screaming, "Don't go! Don't go!" and the sitter is grabbing an arm and a leg and dragging him back in the house and Milton and I are on our way out for another guilt-ridden evening away from the children.

Not all our departures are quite so flamboyant, of course. But—somehow or other—there usually seems to be some sort of drama or trauma connected with leaving the kids at home with a sitter.

The last time we went to a dinner party we received a call right in the middle of the endive salad that Nick had rolled off the upper bunk of his double-decker and rearranged his face. That was about a month after we'd gone away for the weekend and Alexander decided to drink the shoe polish.

Sometimes, it's true, we just go home to a ruined copper pot ("The popcorn got stuck to the bottom") or to no heat ("I guess one of them was fooling with the thermostat"). Sometimes we merely go home to a permanently alienated sitter—"Little *girls* never act that way, and the phonograph doesn't work, and you only have Fresca." Sometimes we even go home to three peacefully sleeping sons and their reasonably serene guardian, only to discover the next morning that the boys plan to move out immediately if "that Janet" ever takes care of them again.

I suppose I should ask myself whether my sitter problems can be traced to some hideous failing in me, my sons, my husband, or my taste in soft drinks. But everyone I know has sitter problems, or used to have them, or most certainly will. The fact is, whenever we put someone else in charge of our children, there are many golden opportunities for aggravation. Some of us get to experience them all.

Many of our problems with sitters seem to have to do with the great discrepancy between the kind of person we want to take care of our kids and the kind we get. All of us, I imagine, have some sort of vision of the ideal mother-substitute for our children. She is warm and loving and patient, firm but never harsh, and relaxed without the slightest hint of neglectfulness. She is the perfect guardian of their bodies, capable of any medical feat from removing splinters to performing a tracheotomy. She is the perfect guardian of their psyches, capable of dealing with any disturbance from temper tantrum to Portnoy's complaint. She is sensitive, tactful, healthy, and always available. And she is so crazy about our children that she's almost embarrassed to be paid for the pleasure of tending them.

Needless to say, there isn't any such person. Furthermore, anyone bearing the faintest resemblance to such a person has been booked until late 1987 by unscrupulous females offering more money, fewer children, and color TV. The rest of us, alas, must learn to work out our conflicting philosophies of child care with lesser mortals—and to deal with plenty of guilt.

I'll explain about guilt.

There you are at your friendly neighborhood theater, watching one of those X-rated movies that the critics have unanimously hailed as "explicit, shocking, depraved," and back at the house your son trips over his shoelace and knocks out a tooth.

Did you remember to tie his laces before you left? Did you remember to tell the sitter to tie his laces? No, you did not. For you were too busy hurrying to get to the movie on time, and if you now have the only toothless toddler in town, it's because you were heartless and irresponsible and probably a sex maniac besides.

Why, our guilty conscience asks us, don't we stay home, which is surely where every *good* mother belongs? By staying home, this guilty conscience assures us, we can prevent all sorts of catastrophes, psychological as well as physical. We can deal intelligently with sibling rivalry, the middle-child syndrome, crime and punishment, and whether or not the twins can wear their cowboy hats and holsters to bed. Our sitter will do her best, of course, but since she isn't Anna Freud she's bound to bungle the job.

We may not be Anna Freud either, but if someone is going to mess up our children we'd just as soon it be us. What, after all, is more important—a son with an unscarred psyche or dinner in Chinatown?

Now if, by any chance, we somehow fail to raise such guilt-ridden questions, we can always count on our kids to do it for us. For children very quickly master the art of inspiring and nurturing guilt feelings in parents who go off to pursue their grown-up pleasures.

My Alexander, for instance, well before he had reached his third birthday, had formulated a guilt-making scheme that could sometimes stall my departure for a good half hour. It involved an almost Chaplinesque gift for miming total despair—bowed shoulders, bowed head, trembling lower lip, and a single tear trickling slowly down one cheek.

"*Now* what's the matter?" I'd ask in my briskest, most no-nonsense voice.

"Oh," he'd reply, barely audibly, "I just feel so sad."

Cookies, hugs, a full three choruses of his favorite song ("Who did? Who did? Who did? Who did? Who did swallow Jo-Jo-Jo-Jo?") lifted the gloom only temporarily. My last sight, as I forced myself out the front door, would be of a broken, brooding figure in a fuzzy yellow Wear-a-Blanket, incapable of knowing joy again.

For kids who dislike making scenes at the door there is always illness—imaginary or real—to fall back on. I know a boy who can muster up a sensational asthma attack on five minutes' notice and another who can reproduce a stomachache with such fidelity that someday he's going to wind up with a wholly unneeded appendectomy. I'm also told about one little girl who, though she never, never complains when her parents plan an evening out, invariably runs a fever—a genuine fever—just as they are putting on their coats.

Many children permit their parents to depart in peace, only to extract full payment later on in the evening. Children who refuse to remember that they stopped wetting the bed two years ago, children who refuse to eat a single morsel of sitter-served food, children who refuse to fall asleep until Mommy and Daddy return, are clearly trying to discourage us from going away.

I should point out, however, that I've not yet encountered any parents so beset with guilt feelings that they've actually given up leaving their children with sitters. I've also noticed that most parents (including Milton and me) tend to become less vulnerable to guilt with our second child than we were with our first. Indeed, by the time we have had our third we may find ourselves scarcely wincing when we're told tearfully, "I hurt myself and you weren't here," or, "The baby-sitter likes Billy better than me." And if an eight-year-old logician should ask in accusing tones, "How can you go out tonight when you just went out last night?" we can stare him down and coldly reply, "It's easy."

But even if we succeed in keeping our guilt under control, we're almost sure to encounter other baby-sitting problems. For instance:

When a highly precise mother is dealing with a highly casual sitter, there is plenty of room for aggravation. The mother says give the baby his last feeding at exactly 6:17. She says give him the blue blanket with the white doggies and not the white blanket with the blue doggies. She says open his left bedroom window just two and a half inches.

None of these things happen, of course. The baby gets a 9:30 feeding, the wrong doggies, and either too much air or no air at all. The mother concludes that the sitter is unreliable. The sitter concludes that the mother is uptight.

When a highly indulgent mother turns her children over to a more conservative type, there is also aggravation. I frankly thought that the superpermissive school of child raising had been laughed out of existence years ago. But sitters still tell me about households where kids are encouraged to express themselves in every way, from throwing a glass of milk if they're feeling hostile to staying up all night if they're not feeling sleepy. These households tend to have a large turnover in baby-sitters. Either the sitters refuse to return again at any price, or they are not invited back after discouraging an excessive act of self-expression.

Misunderstandings between parents and sitters and between sitters and sittees are yet another form of aggravation.

One of my friends recalls telling her sitter, "Be sure the children enjoy themselves and don't worry about the house." She returned to find chewing gum on the sofa, finger paints on the curtains, melting chocolate ice cream on the rug, and a broken chandelier—the result of an energetic ball game—in the living room. "No child," she informed her sitter rather grimly, "has to be *that* happy."

Nick had a little misunderstanding last year with his sitter when he cheerfully informed her that his Uncle Henry was a vegetable. Since she was a very sensitive young lady she kept muttering things like "Oh, the poor man," and "I don't think it's nice of you to laugh about it," while Nick kept saying how funny he thought it was. The sitter grew more annoyed and Nick more baffled and hurt until our oldest boy relieved the tension by explaining that the reason Uncle Henry was a vegetable was that he never ate meat.

If a mother is the worrying kind, she is bound to be aggravated by her sitter because no sitter, in her eyes, could possibly display the proper concern for her children's welfare.

The average mother, for example, might prepare for

possible crises by leaving a list of emergency numbers plus a number where she and her husband can be reached. The worrying mother also leaves a list, but it is at least three times longer, and that's only the beginning. The worrier then goes on to explain what to do in case of croup or nuclear holocaust, and finishes by utterly unnerving the sitter with detailed instructions on how to escape from rabid dogs, fight off kidnapers, and remove marbles from the throats of choking four-year-olds.

In my ten years as a parent I've managed to aggravate and be aggravated by various baby-sitters in just about all these ways, and so have most of the mothers I know. We've had our maddening moments with the teen-ager who sits on Saturday nights and with the lady who comes to clean every other Thursday. We've had them with the friend with whom we've arranged one of those I'll-take-Robby-on-Mondays-if-you'll-take-Amy-on-Wednesdays baby-sitting exchange programs. And we've had them (God knows we've had them!) with that expert on how to raise our children better than we can—the grandmother.

A lot of mothers complain that teen-aged sitters are too sloppy or too hip for their taste. The slobs, they say, invariably put the kids to bed with the remains of Ho Hos and milk all over their faces. The hip ones, they grumble, teach their kids to question the relevance of everything from an elementary school education to a mother. They may even teach them, or so one appalled parent solemnly informed me, the proper way to roll a joint.

As for the cleaning lady as baby-sitter, she troubles mothers in quite a different way. If one of us wants to leave a child in her charge while we slip off to shop and maybe have our hair done, we probably needn't bother checking out her smoking habits or her ideology. Chances are she'll be too busy trying to straighten up the house to indoctrinate our child—so busy, in fact, that she'll plunk him in front of TV from *Today* to the six o'clock news. Now perhaps this is against everything we believe in, but we assure ourselves we'll compensate by filling the rest of our kid's days with cultural enrichment. Perhaps this is against everything we believe in, but we remind ourselves that so are a lot of other things we manage to live with. And perhaps this issue is considerably less than burning, but who is above agonizing about it?

When it comes to trading sitting days with a friend, all I can say is, watch out! There are many women who dearly love each other, women who share identical views on everything from politics to Robert Redford. But let them take care of each other's children for a day, or even for an afternoon, and they may turn into lifelong enemies.

I've had one enlightening experience along these lines. It was with the mother of a monster I'll call Daniel, who obtained a certain pleasure from biting Anthony (then about two and a half) and belting him about the head with lethal objects. At Daniel's house his mother pursued a hands-off, they-must-work-these-things-out-for-themselves policy. Anthony returned from each visit bruised and tearful. At my house I pursued an antiviolence policy—first by explaining, next by scolding, and finally by whacking Daniel on the bottom. He also returned home bruised and tearful.

Luckily, Dan's mother and I had the good sense to call off our baby-sitting exchange after three increasingly strained weeks. And while I acknowledge that many women manage this sort of arrangement beautifully, I also suspect that we're a lot touchier on the subject of child raising than we are on politics—or Robert Redford.

But if we want to plumb new depths of touchiness, all we need do is turn over our children to their grandmother, whose services as a sitter can be simultaneously the cheapest and costliest available.

We all know the advantages of a baby-sitting grandma.

(37)

She loves our children at least as deeply as we do, and she worries about them at least twice as much. She can outindulge the most overindulgent among us, and she can easily outprotect the most overprotective. With her in charge, our child will never have a dirty face, will never walk in the rain without his galoshes, and will never fall from the top of the jungle gym because Grandma will be standing right below him, holding on to his ankles.

The trouble with a grandmother, of course, is that she is also somebody's mother—ours or our husband's—with all the tensions, conflicts, and resentments such relationships imply. Furthermore, being a mother, she feels that she has already irrefutably proved her skills as a child raiser. If, then, we try to persuade her that our son doesn't need three sweaters under his snowsuit, she can quickly point out that *her* son always wore three sweaters under his snowsuit and was, as a result, so healthy that he never missed a day of kindergarten.

Grandmothers may make similar assertions about a host of other issues, from pacifiers ("They'll ruin his teeth. I never gave my children pacifiers and not one of them needed braces") to a hot breakfast ("It'll keep him going all day. What kind of mother wouldn't cook oatmeal for her child?"). Some of us may have to ask ourselves if we are willing, when Grandmother is the sitter, to let her handle our children her way, even when her way is not ours.

On the other hand we might ask ourselves whether we're inclined to give a grandmother an unduly hard time about her baby-sitting methods simply because we figure—in our modernized, psychologized sophistication—that she couldn't possibly know what's right. I still remember with some embarrassment the typed instructions I presented to my mother-in-law the evening she first sat for us. Included were handy child-care items like "Smile frequently while feeding bottle" and "Place all fatal medications safely out of reach." Thinking back on it now, I am amazed that my mother-in-law didn't smile frequently, hand me back my kid, and place *herself* safely out of reach.

Even when we don't collide with Grandma on her child-raising methods, we may find reasons for aggravation if in her baby-sitting capacity she displays tendencies toward martyrdom or one-upmanship.

The martyred grandmother is one whose chief joy in tending our children seems to derive from letting us know how exhausting it all is. She arrives, gives the kids a kiss, and sinks painfully into a chair, wordlessly conveying the impression that she will be departing at the end of the evening by ambulance. Some of the more committed martyrs will insist that we leave the kids with them for a weekend or even longer. But when we phone to find out how things are going we are sure to hear plenty about high blood pressure, swollen ankles, and sleepless nights, inevitably coupled with a gallant "I'll manage somehow."

Quite different, but certainly no less maddening, is the one-upmanship grandmother who tells us, "What do you mean, Jimmy is a whiner? He certainly never whines when he's with me." Nor can she understand why they won't eat the string beans we cook when they're simply wild about hers.

In our own family, whenever my mother used to take over the sitting, I found I had an unusual kind of complaint —my mother as a baby-sitter was just about perfect. If you don't think that's reason to gripe, listen to this:

During school vacations the children were invited to spend a week with her in New Jersey, a week filled from dawn to dark with trips to toy stores, trips to the zoo, trips to feed the ducks at a nearby pond, trips to the new children's movie at Radio City. Cheerfully, even enthusiastically, she read *Goodnight Moon* to Alexander five times in a row, helped Nicholas Elmer-glue his model cars, and played endless games of checkers with Anthony. Together they sledded down hills and baked tons of cookies. Nobody ever wanted to come home.

But they did. After seven days of Paradise my children returned to plain, ordinary, grumpy, preoccupied me. The reentry problem was shattering. The kids kept asking what wonderful plans and pleasures I had arranged for them today, and I kept telling them I wasn't their social director. It was only after considerable scolding and weeping that we all finally got used to each other again.

Now, if we have to have a baby-sitting problem, a perfect grandmother is certainly the best kind. But since we're bound to have most of the other kinds too, we might as well be prepared for guilt and worry, misunderstandings and complaints, and profound disagreements on how a child should be raised.

We might also start recognizing the fact that we are probably just as aggravating to our sitters as vice versa, and that our children will doubtless survive both them—and us.

V

Single Wasn't So Swell

❧❦❧

For a couple of years before I married Milton—before those fights and those kids and those baby-sitters—I dwelled in the wicked city of New York. I was there to burn my candle at both ends, live life to the hilt, and do all of those other wild, delicious things that my mother would never allow me to do in New Jersey.

Ah, those were the golden days, I always tell Milton.

Or, as I asked myself only last week, were they?

It was one of those weeks when all three kids had come down simultaneously with a stomach virus and the chicken pox, and my husband kept pointing out dust on the blinds and the baseboards, and my four-year-old drove his tricycle over my wristwatch, and my husband remarked that my dinners were quite uninventive, and my in-laws phoned me to tell me I never phoned them, and I said to myself, "For this a person gets married?"

What, I asked myself, am I doing here with all these crabs and complainers, instead of lying in the arms of ardent lovers? Why am I stuffing potato peels down the Disposal when I could be dancing in the dark with a titled nobleman or a rock musician or the world's greatest living Shakespearean actor or the world's greatest living revolutionary or an international playboy and sex symbol?

Wasn't it better, I asked myself, back when I was single, back when I lived on my own in Greenwich Village, back when I could roam heedlessly through spring rains with a pounding heart and a throbbing pulse and lots of agony and ecstasy? Wasn't it better before?

The answer is no.

Not "I don't think so."

Not "It's hard to say."

Just . . . plain . . . no.

Having sifted through my youthful (and harrowing) memories, I can now make this unequivocal declaration: visit upon me a dozen cases of stomach virus, visit upon me a year of the chicken pox, but please don't ask me to ever be single again.

First of all, there were never any noblemen. Instead there was Herbie Prince, whose only claim to nobility was his name. Poor Herbie, I well recall, was a hypochondriac, and we never got to roam heedlessly through spring rains because he was terrified of developing bronchitis. He's the only man I ever heard of who used to demonstrate his devotion by showing up, not with daffodils but with a jar of one-a-day vitamins.

As for living on my own in Greenwich Village, I'm afraid I never had any of those searingly beautiful—or was it beautifully searing?—experiences I claimed to be looking for when I moved away from the suburbs of New Jersey. Although I'd intended to be doing things like dashing off to orgies, smoking marijuana, and having dark encounters with suicidal poets, I always wound up doing things like watching hockey matches with somebody's brother's roommate from the Bronx.

"If I were the kind of person who toasted marshmallows," a suicidal poet once informed me, "you're the kind of person I'd toast them with."

Clearly I was doing something wrong.

It's true that my village apartment was fully equipped with mobiles, bullfight posters, a fireplace, roaches, and the other paraphernalia of bohemian life. But it somehow failed to emanate a mood of abandon. Furthermore, it was also equipped with top sheets, a vacuum cleaner, and several cans of lilac-scented air freshener, delivered to me in person by my mother, along with one deeply heartfelt bit of advice: get married.

Well, maybe she didn't put it quite so crudely. But she was always full of the most poignant stories about the 24-year-old old maid ("On Saturdays she sits all alone in her walk-up and watches *The Late Show*") and the 26-year-old old maid ("Every night she weeps into her pillow") and the 30-year-old old maid ("Nine years ago last May she turned down a dentist and nobody else has ever asked her again").

The moral of these tales was very clear. If I didn't want to wind up an outcast on the shores of love, I should find a fellow.

A fellow to give me a ring and a couple of children, a paycheck each week, a vacation once a year.

A fellow who if, God forbid, I should catch pneumonia, would drive in the snow to the druggist for antibiotics.

A fellow to guarantee that I'd never watch television unaccompanied or dampen my Springmaid sheets with lonely tears or live out my life as that most unfortunate of creatures, a woman nobody picked to be his mate.

Look, you have to remember that I was single just before the invention of the sex revolution and Women's Lib, just before everyone started writing about the decline and fall of marriage and the family. No one ever encouraged me to have dozens of guilt-free affairs or to aspire to the presidency of GM. The plan was starkly simple: enjoy yourself in college—but make certain you're engaged by the senior prom.

Girls who somehow fumbled this opportunity went on to take a graduate course in husband-hunting.

Oh, it wasn't *called* husband-hunting. Certainly not! Our official position was that we adored our freedom, were crazy about sharpening pencils in publishing houses, and had better things to do than find a man. That *had* to be our official position. Marital opportunities, we'd been assured, increased in direct proportion to one's nonchalance.

As a matter of fact I do have one friend, Laurie, who was, in her single days, really and truly nonchalant and who still insists that she entered marriage much against her will.

Laurie never suffered from find-a-fellow frenzy. She was that ultimate thing to be at 21—Very Popular.

Laurie was the type of girl whom high-cheekboned men with no money but sensitive souls taught about socialism and modern art. She was the type whom rich older men introduced to sweetbreads and Beaujolais at restaurants so famous that even her folks back in Wilkes-Barre knew the names. She was the type who, when *My Fair Lady* was the smash-hit musical on Broadway, saw it six different times with six different dates.

I wasn't that type at all. Nor did I possess that precious ace in the hole that a girl like Laurie always seemed to have, a faithful Paul or George or Max or Larry who, if all else failed, would take her out on New Year's Eve—or marry her.

So I husband-hunted. Discreetly, of course. But that's what it really was.

I'd go to a beach, for instance, with a copy of *The Brothers Karamazov,* as if all I'd ever need to make me happy was sand and sea, the sun, and Dostoevski. If I was lucky, a bronze god would eventually perch himself on the edge of my blanket and say something ingratiating like "You're getting a sun blister on your lip." I was supposed to snap back with some very clever line to demonstrate my terrific sense of humor, after which I had exactly five minutes to show him how adorable and charming I was so he'd —please, dear God—ask me out to dinner.

I hunted at parties too, arriving in dresses designed to inspire desire and asking ridiculous, breathlessly interested questions like "Tell me, what exactly *is* a tax shelter?" (As my mother always said, "Be a good listener. After you're married you'll have plenty of time to talk.")

How I hated those parties! I didn't scintillate. I had no charisma. I was nervous and ill at ease. "Who is that glorious creature sipping vodka?" was never something anyone asked about me.

I suppose I didn't have to go to those parties. I suppose I could have rinsed out bras instead. I suppose I could have savored the pleasures of privacy—the pleasures, for instance, of soaking in a bubble bath for hours without three children kicking down the door.

But I'm kidding myself. Even when I did wind up soaking in bathtubs I certainly wouldn't say I *savored* it. I was more likely chewing nervously on a cuticle and hoping someone would call me for Saturday night. Let me tell you a secret: privacy's only nice if you're sure it will end.

So forget all that nonsense about how swell it was not to have to clean the apartment and how swell it was not to

(*45*)

have to cook dinner and how swell it was not to have to share your closet with a man who dumped loafers on top of your new suede boots and hung his jacket on top of your best chiffon. That's the kind of swell that never seemed swell at the time.

Another thing that wasn't so swell was sex—or, to be more precise, the avoidance thereof. I'll admit it was awfully flattering to evoke all that naked longing and raw passion—but not on the second date. Fellows I scarcely knew, fellows who were still unaware that green was my favorite color and Rose my middle name, were forever attempting to sweep me into bed, while I, with the skill of a California surfer, fought to maintain a vertical position.

Oh Lord, the agony of those abortive seduction scenes, with the would-you-mind-taking-your-hand-away-from-where-you've-just-put-it line, and the it's-not-that-I'm-rejecting-you-personally line, and the just-because-I-invited-you-up-for-coffee-doesn't-mean-I'm-that-kind-of-a-girl line, and the we-don't-really-know-each-other line, and the if-you-don't-cut-that-out-immediately-I-am-going-to-scream line.

I repeat, sex was a terribly serious matter back in my single days. Did he love me? Did he respect me? Would he talk about me? With questions like that, virtue tended to be more appealing than vice.

As rejected lovers stalked off into the night they would hurl the most unfriendly reproaches behind them.

Like the psychological reproach: "Have you ever discussed your frigidity with an analyst?"

And the man-of-the-world reproach: "You are still a child, my dear. You are not yet a real woman."

And the great-lover reproach: "Baby, you'll never know what you've missed."

Meanwhile my mother would phone every day from

New Jersey, to keep in touch with my health, well-being, and progress.

Perhaps, she would tell me, I ought to change my job, since there weren't any available men in my office. (Marge went to work in a bank and she met an accountant.)

Or perhaps I should try a new hairdo and lose a few pounds. (Louise down the street switched to bangs and now goes with a teacher.)

Or perhaps I should save up my money and go on a cruise. (On a cruise, once upon a time, Lillian Fine, a legendary figure in my life, met and subsequently married the owner of a supermarket chain. Northern New Jersey has not yet recovered from this triumph.)

Mostly, however, my mother would phone for the purpose of pushing some crafty matchmaking scheme of her own.

"Belle's boy," she'd alert me, "was over to visit last weekend, and darling, believe me, I've never seen such a doll. Beautiful blue twinkly eyes. Marvelous manners. And he's one of the biggest chiropodists in town."

Then she'd concoct a plot to bring us together—some elaborate and transparent arrangement involving chance encounters at the swim club they all belonged to or at the delicatessen they went to on Sunday nights.

"Or perhaps," she would blandly suggest, "I should throw a small brunch and very, very casually invite him. I feel in my bones you two would hit it off."

As a matter of fact, *everyone* had a someone with whom, in their bones, they were sure I'd hit it off. And while some of those someones turned out to be a cowpuncher from Joplin, Missouri, and a mystic who found our astrological signs incompatible, and an intern whose ideal of physical perfection was short, blond, and blue-eyed (I'm dark and tall and all I could do was stoop), I was still grateful to be what is known in the trade as fixed-up.

Don't forget that in my single days a nice girl couldn't meet fellows on buses or subways, in theater lobbies, bars, or in the park. Picking up strangers, my mother had frequently warned me, could only lead to murder, rape, or worse.

Beaches, for reasons I never quite understood, were exempt from this rule. One girl friend of mine also exempted the Museum of Modern Art on the dubious grounds that killers and rapists did not hang around Cézannes. But that still left our stalking grounds exceedingly limited.

And so when my friends Ruth and Gary would ask me to dinner to meet what they always swore was the man of my dreams, I always went. They set the scene with candles, wine, and Segovia, but somehow it never came out very romantic.

You see, Ruth would want to make sure that David (the man of my dreams) knew what a prize was sitting within his grasp, so she'd say things like "You think this roast is delicious. You should taste Judy's. She also reads a lot and deeply loves nature."

And then Gary, who wanted to make sure that I knew I was sitting across from the biggest catch in New York, would say things like "You think Edward Bennett Williams is a brilliant lawyer? You should hear David. He also likes to sail and enjoys a good laugh."

They were only trying to help, of course, but the result was that I'd spend all evening reeling off the names of best sellers to show how well-read I was and David would spend all evening chuckling merrily over every dumb remark to show how much he enjoyed a good laugh. By 11 P.M. we couldn't stand each other.

Still, every now and then I would find true love—or whatever I was calling true love those days. It was beautiful; it was tender; but most of all it was dreadfully

(*48*)

exhausting. Among the blessings I count when I count my blessings is that I'll never have to go through that again.

Oh, boy, do I remember those young loves! Intense exchanges over the Chianti. Fever-pitch feelings on the Staten Island Ferry. Turbulent emotions in Central Park. Urgent questions like "Is our relationship stagnating?" We analyzed each other's dreams and borrowed each other's toothbrush and I swore that even if he went to jail for 20 years I'd never leave him, and he swore that even if someone threw acid in my face, he'd never leave me.

It was most reassuring.

Maybe young love was lovely while it lasted, but I'm afraid it never lasted too long. All my single years, it seems to me, consisted of 15 minutes of perfect rapture and 15 weeks of perfect misery.

"You didn't call."

"Who says I have to call?"

"Where were you last night?"

"Who are you—my mother?"

"I love you."

Silence.

"I love you."

More silence.

How did I have the strength?

The end of a romance always seemed to leave me with bleeding gums and pimples on my chin, in addition to the standard signs of heartbreak like sleepless nights. But after I'd persuaded myself that he had never been the right man for me in the first place, and after I'd persuaded myself that despite rejections and physical afflictions I wasn't the most repulsive girl in the East, I'd go out looking for love and marriage again.

But I didn't *want* to look.

What I wanted was to be awakened one hot July morning at 1 A.M., and this old friend from college would be on the telephone, and he'd say he just missed his plane and could he come over, and I'd say yes.

And then he'd arrive, looking tan and very great, and we'd talk and talk until dawn and never feel tired, and afterward he'd write and ask could he see me again, and I'd say yes.

And then we would go to a football game, which I hate (but I didn't with him); and then on a camping trip, which I also hate (but I didn't with him); and then, one night, on our way to my apartment, he'd stop the car and ask did I want lots of children; and I'd know that he was asking to marry me and that I'd say yes.

And I did.

VI

The Woman to Whom He Is Married

❧⚜❧

The girl that Milton proposed to all those years ago isn't the woman he's married to today. The faults which, blinded by love, he didn't notice—and which I had no intention of pointing out—have, as faults tend to do, become apparent. And furthermore, like everyone else, I've changed.

Once upon a time I was an idealistic young woman who scorned material possessions and had never even heard of things like rinse cycles.

Today I am the owner of an automatic ice-maker, a 12-speed blender, and a self-cleaning oven.

Once upon a time all I couldn't live without was Milton.

But today what I also can't live without is my hair drier,

my air conditioner, and the fellow who fixes my television set.

How did this happen? How did I stop being this terribly pure person who considered matching sheets and pillowcases decadent, and turn into this terribly decadent person who can't open peas without the electric can opener?

I'm not quite sure. It was certainly not in my plan. When, early in our marriage, my parents offered to buy us a washer-drier, I remember with what self-righteousness I declined. "How vulgar!" I told them. "How pretentious. How bourgeois."

A little bit later, however, after our first child was born, I found I not only needed a washer-drier but was likely to sink into a black depression if it broke down. I blush to admit that my current list of emergency numbers includes the Police Department, the Fire Department, and the repair department at G.E.

Okay, I sold out. It started a decade ago with the washing machine, and today I'm completely plugged in. In my universe, power to the people has come to mean an electric blanket, an electric toothbrush, and the Disposal.

These days, when a fuse blows, I can't even take care of my children, because like most desperate mothers I count on TV to keep them diverted and me sane. (Needless to say, it was also not part of my plan to be screaming at my eight-year-old, "No, I will not read you William Shakespeare. Get out of here and go watch *Spider Man*.")

Oh, I sold out all right. And not just to machines, but to many other possessions and comforts as well, possessions and comforts I considered beneath contempt back in the days when my mother's favorite household hint was "Buy wool."

But now I buy wool. And I use vases instead of empty mayonnaise jars, enameled ashtrays instead of seashells, doormats instead of old newspapers—and the high-priced spread. My sheets and pillowcases match, and so do my forks, knives, and spoons. I wish I didn't want them to, but I do.

Sometimes, in the middle of the night, I wake and ask myself whether I'm a better person because my telephones are color-coordinated.

And then I ask myself, what kind of question is that to ask in the middle of the night?

Since color-coordinated phones cost more than black ones, I find that I'm spending much more these days than I did in my uncontaminated youth. So another question I ask myself in the middle of the night is "How can I save money?"

Now I've read lots of articles lately about how the rich economize by hoarding old pieces of string and turning off the lights in the upstairs drawing room.

But since I don't know what to *do* with all that string, and since I don't have any drawing rooms to darken, I must find other ways of saving money.

Some of my best economizing occurs at clearance sales, to which I am drawn by those ads that say "Prices Unmercifully Slashed," and "Everything's Got to Go," and, more recently, "Selling Out—Owner Has Repudiated Materialism and Is Moving to Commune."

While it's true that these clearances sometimes attempt to deceive (like the time I found an 80-piece set of stainless reduced from $125 to $3 per piece), I've also come across some mind-blowing bargains.

At the Threads for Heads clothing shop, for instance, I once discovered an African Monkey coat, mercilessly slashed from $80 to $34.95. Although there were some nasty rumors that the African Monkey was actually Washington Rat, I believe these were started by a jealous competitor—the Duds for Studs clothing shop across the street.

I also once found, at a modern-furniture sale, a triumph of twentieth-century know-how—a combination end table, floor lamp, eternal flame, and electric broom. I won't take the time to explain how this clever thing worked, but you have my word that at $94, mercilessly slashed from $176, it was quite a steal.

What makes my going to these sales so economical, however, is that I *don't* buy these bargains, tempting though they may be. By always asking myself, "Could you, if you had to, live without it?" I've saved our family a fortune.

Another way I save is by spending, whenever possible, not *real* money but what I call "found money." Found money, I should explain, is money that, except for extraordinary circumstances, I wouldn't have—so I'm not really spending anything at all.

An example of found money is the $5 I get back when, by mistake, I pay $37 for something that only costs $32. And it's the $2 that's left when I budget $60 for the supermarket and I only had to spend $58. And it's the extra $34.95 I wind up with when I don't buy that African Monkey coat.

Still another economy device I rely on is quantity shopping. You know—two cans of carrot paste for 29¢, four for 58¢, eight for $1.16, and 100 for $14.50. One problem with quantity shopping, however, is that each can of carrot paste—which is not a popular item around our house—lasts for several years, and I may not live long enough to enjoy my bargain. Another problem is that Milton keeps insisting that I save no more money buying 100 cans than I do buying two.

I don't believe it.

But even if he's right, I won't let him discourage my economies.

As my mother often said, it's the thought that counts.

In addition to becoming materialistic, and spending more money than I should, I am also a rotten dancer, a rotten driver, a worrier, a coward, and a nag. And sometimes (when my husband's out of town) I serve instant mashed potatoes to the kids.

But if I don't seem to be depressed by the flaws in my nature, it's because I believe they're going to go away. Not in March. Or in August. Or November. But on January one of the brave new year.

For inside the old inadequate me is a new fantastic me, waiting to burst into bloom. Or so it seems, every December 31, as I contemplate the as-yet-unblemished year that lies ahead and draw up my annual list of resolutions.

I recognize, of course, that New Year's resolutions are thought to be childish. And unsophisticated. And the kind of thing that grown-ups just don't do. But every time the hands of the clock edge toward midnight, the me-I-could-be seems as real as the me-that-I-am, and before I know it I'm writing my list once again.

This year, however, is different. This year it's going to work. This year, I'm proud to say, I've given up my dreams of total perfection. Perfection, I've decided, is unattainable. Practically perfect is going to suit me just fine.

Which is why you'll no longer find on my list of New Year's resolutions any rash resolves to study the harpsichord, master mathematics, or go to the National Gallery of Art once a week for the pure and noble purpose of relating to Rembrandt. Furthermore, I've at last quit harboring the hope, clung to for many and many a year, of becoming so magnificent a mother that my sons would be certain to score at least 100 percent on their Psychological Adjustment and Happiness Test.

Oh yes, I'm more sensible now. I know about me and music, about me and math, about me and motherhood. And I also know that though I could certainly find the time to look at Rembrandts, and though I genuinely admire the folks who do, I myself would really rather not. The fact is —and it's terrible to confess—that I'd much rather see a Woody Allen movie than a Rembrandt.

But having faced these sorrowful truths about my nature, and having learned to live with them, I am now prepared to concentrate on more plausible improvements in my character. Plausible, that is, to me. There are some people around—namely my husband—who responded to my list of resolutions with great noisy roars of cynical laughter.

But we'll see who has the last laugh—and in the meantime, undeterred, I hereby resolve:

1. *I will display grace under pressure.* Grace under pressure is what Hemingway heroes have, and what I do not have at all. When a Hemingway hero is pierced through the heart by a maddened bull in Spain or chewed in half by a lion in the green hills of Africa, does he make a scene? Certainly not. As his life's blood ebbs away, he smiles gallantly into the eyes of his weeping admirers and says, without a quaver, "It's only a scratch."

In my universe, however, nothing is only a scratch. I mean, show me a scratch and I'll come right back with intimations of tourniquets and blood poisoning. Throughout my life I have specialized in (a) how to convert annoyance into agony, and (b) how to then completely go to pieces.

On a car trip, for instance, when it's suppertime, and I say I'm starving, and my husband says he won't stop at *this*

Howard Johnson's he'll stop at the next one, and then we drive for 75 miles and there's still no next one, I am not too likely to show much grace about it. Instead, I'll clutch my stomach and moan about hunger pangs. After which I'll rub my temples and sigh about headaches. After which I might announce that I'm going to faint. By the time we've finally arrived at a restaurant, I could even be capable of claiming that the anguish I've endured has destroyed my appetite and he should please just go ahead and eat without me.

That is not a shining example of grace under pressure.

For years I've tried to explain to my husband that, despite such behavior, I was confident that I could, at any time, rise to a Hemingway-hero kind of crisis. It was just the Howard Johnson's kind of crisis I couldn't take. Recently, however, I've decided that in the life of a housewife there are few maddened bulls and murderous lions and lots of delayed dinners—and that if I plan to develop grace under pressure I'd better start small.

2. *I will become inwardly serene.* Inner serenity is a lot like grace under pressure except that it's all going on inside where people might not notice and give you credit. I understand, though, that once you become inwardly serene, you don't want credit.

3. *I will acquire élan.* My friend Joannie has five small kids and tons of élan. Take last week, when her husband phoned at lunchtime from the office and said, "My old college roommate just came into town. Why don't you call up 50 or 60 people and we'll throw him a nice little cocktail party tonight."

Now my girl friend Joannie didn't hang up on her husband. And she didn't say okay through gritted teeth. Nor did she even merely remain unruffled. Not Joannie. "Terrific!" she said, and she wasn't being sarcastic. "I'm really feeling just in the mood for a party."

The thing about Joannie is, she's always in the mood—for a party, or a 20-mile hike, or packing up the entire family in two hours flat and taking off for the jungles of South America. Most of the ventures that I would call either impossible, or terrifying, or grotesque, or utterly insane, my girl friend Joannie calls fun.

Now that's élan, and I want some. I want, when someone phones and says let's go, to go, instead of always replying that my coat isn't back from the cleaners, and the children have an appointment with the dentist, and my hair is too much of a mess, and who'll water the plants. So far I've spent an entire lifetime being the type of person who, had the world's most seductive man whispered in my ear, "Come with me to the Casbah," would have whispered right back in *his* ear, "But I don't think my smallpox shot is up to date."

It's true that in the New Year, what with Milton and my boys, I probably still couldn't say I'd come to the Casbah. But at least let me have enough élan to not let my passport expire.

4. *I will stop liking gossip.* Please note that I've chosen my words quite carefully. I'm not promising to *give up* gossip—a lofty but hopeless aspiration. I'm only saying that from now on, when Martha Lewin tells me what happened the night that Harriet's husband and Stanley's wife went down to the basement together, I'll try very hard to wish she hadn't told me.

5. *My modesty and self-effacement will stun you.* Yesterday morning the butcher winked at me over the counter and said, "That's an awful cute dress you're wearing." By yesterday evening I had repeated the story to eight different people. I would have repeated it to 11 different people, but three, unfortunately, weren't home when I phoned. I also figured that, as long as I was chatting with these people, I might as well mention that Nick had been

named the third best speller in third grade and that an extremely famous New York interior decorator had been quite impressed with my new end table.

You know what that's called, don't you? That's called bragging. It's called bragging no matter how well you disguise it and no matter how tricky and sneaky and subtle you attempt to be. The plain fact is that when you call up someone for the sole purpose of letting them know that you're hungered after, and that your children are brilliant, and that your taste in home furnishings is impeccable, you are *not* being modest and self-effacing.

Some women are great at self-effacement. Lynn from down the street, for instance, not only wouldn't dream of repeating a compliment—she wouldn't dream of accepting one. If you say, "Your little girl is pretty," she'll come right back with, "Who—that dumb-looking kid?" If you admire a painting on her wall, she'll tell you, "It's nothing but a cheap reproduction." And if you mention how lovely her roses are, she'll reply that they're dying of blight.

By this time, of course, Lynn has managed to persuade you that your judgment stinks and you just don't know what's good. That may be carrying self-effacement too far —but I think I'll give it a try.

6. *Compassion will well from my heart.* It isn't that I've got a heart of stone, but on the other hand I'm not my cousin Eleanor, who regards her husband's merest case of sniffles as a grand opportunity to smother him in homemade soup and tenderness.

"Poor darling," she'll say, plumping up the pillows on the bed into which he's retired at her insistence, "how you must be suffering."

I think I love my husband every bit as much as Eleanor loves hers, but I'm not nearly so good at feeling sorry for him. When he catches a cold, I tend to suspect that he's done so just to aggravate me, and that he's a hell of a lot more healthy than he claims. "Your temperature," I'll reluctantly concede, "is 103, but I'm sure the thermometer is high."

I'm afraid I'm not much better with the kids. "Just because it's little bumps, and itches," I once insisted, hustling them out the door, "doesn't have to mean it's chicken pox."

Except it was.

But all of this will change in the coming year, when my cousin Eleanor will seem like a cold-blooded monster compared to me. I'm getting a new thermometer, a first-aid book, the large economy jar of vitamin C, and some soup recipes. I want everyone to look to me for compassion.

7. *I will turn into a darling daughter-in-law.* I suppose that there's no need for me to become violent when my mother-in-law gently suggests that cream wax is better than spray wax. But I do.

I suppose I ought to remember her birthday on the day it occurs and not six or seven weeks later. But I don't.

I also suppose that when she empties one of my ashtrays I needn't conclude that she is tacitly implying that I'm a lazy slob of a housewife, unworthy of her handsome only son.

But whenever she empties an ashtray, I get huffy. And whenever she tells me to call her next week, I get huffy. And whenever she says my new hairstyle looks nice, I get huffy, because I presume that she means that my *old* hairstyle looked awful.

Furthermore, as long as I'm confessing, I might as well admit that while her pot roast always comes out moist and tender, and mine always comes out dry and tough, I cannot bring myself to ask her for her recipe—even though my husband says I should. Or maybe it's *because* he says I should.

So, as you can see, I'm not exactly a mother-in-law's delight. But next year I intend to mend my ways. It has suddenly struck me that, having three sons, I am probably destined to someday have three daughters-in-law. And let's face it—I'd hate to get one like me.

8. *I won't hold any grudges anymore.* On October 27, 1962, at precisely 4:30 P.M., my husband was supposed to meet me downtown so we could pick out a rug for the bedroom.

He forgot.

I, however, have never forgotten waiting in Carpets and Rugs till closing time—certain that my beloved Milton was dead. (If he had merely been critically injured, I told myself, he'd have phoned the department store and said so.) In the intervals when I wasn't positive he was dead, I was positive that he'd shrewdly removed me from the scene so he could steal home, pack a bag, and slip out of the country with his secretary.

All told, it was an emotionally strenuous afternoon.

I'm not denying that Milton was subsequently full of profound remorse, or that he apologized quite handsomely and often. Furthermore, I'll quickly concede that, in the years which followed, it has never happened again. And yet, for all of those years, whenever we're meeting someplace and he's five minutes late, I remind him of Carpets and Rugs in '62.

"I can't help it," I sweetly explain. "You shattered my trust."

But, when the old year is done, I'm done holding grudges. I resolve to learn to forget as well as forgive. I resolve to stop being the type who can never recall my area code or my zip code but can always recall, with brooding photographic precision, the slightest of slights.

In other words, I will stop remembering the time that one of the car-pool mothers told me that my kids should bathe more often. And I will stop remembering the time that my neighbor's husband didn't say hello. And I will stop remembering the time that my own treacherous husband, right in front of me, told my sister her legs were nicer than mine.

Comes December 31, when the clock strikes 12, I swear I'll stop remembering these things. But not—by God—a single second earlier.

9. *I will not envy Silvia Krauss anymore.* In every woman's life there's a Silvia Krauss, and I've got mine. The trouble with Silvia is that in addition to being beautiful, brilliant, sexy, well-organized, and a wonderful mother, she is so incredibly nice that you cannot hate her. Whatever I have done, she has done better—not that she'd ever tell me, but I know. I keep searching for flaws in her character, in order to stop from feeling so inadequate, but—I regret to report—there aren't any.

So, in the year ahead, Silvia Krauss will become my dearest friend. Her virtues will fill me with joy instead of despair. And maybe, if I stick to all my other resolutions, Silvia Krauss will begin to envy *me*.

10. *I will achieve a sense of perspective.* One 98° F Saturday last summer the air conditioning went, and so did the dishwasher. Also, Alexander remembered how to lock that tricky lock on our bathroom door, and then forgot how to unlock it. Also, Nick and his buddy Chris, in the course of transporting a pitcher of lemonade from the kitchen to their sidewalk lemonade stand, slipped on a baseball and spilled it all over my sofa. They then wiped up the sticky mess with my recently purchased $17 blouse, which, they both assured me, looked just like a dustrag.

In addition, I got trapped on the phone for over an hour with the aunt who always says things like "He's awfully small for his age." And then Milton pointed out three new gray hairs I might otherwise not have noticed. And then the neighbor's cat that we were taking care of for the weekend escaped while the boys were selling lemonade, so that I found myself—as the sun blazed overhead—walking up the block screaming, "Here, kitty, kitty."

I was not amused.

Next year, however, I will find such events hilariously funny. The reason I'll find them hilariously funny is that I'll have achieved a sense of perspective. "My husband loves me," I'll say, "and I've got three wonderful boys. What else do I want?"

I can tell you right now that what else I want is—among other things—no more lemonade on my couch or my blouse. However, this is because I don't yet have the capacity to perceive what mature folks would call "the larger picture."

But during the New Year, I'm sure, I'll get perspective.

And grace under pressure.

Élan.

And those other things too.

You can see that I'm not insisting on perfection. For, as I mentioned earlier, practically perfect is going to suit me just fine.

VII

The Other Women

❧§§❧

No matter how perfect—or practically perfect—a wife may be, she always has to watch out for the Other Woman. The Other Woman, according to my definition, is anyone able to charm my husband, amuse my husband, attract my husband, or occupy his wholehearted interest for more than 30 seconds straight.

Am I being unreasonable? Am I being irrational? Am I being jealous? You bet I am.

Over on the other side of the room there is a 19-year-old girl with long hair parted down the middle, and a clingy dress about an inch shorter than her hair, and the clear-eyed, fresh-faced look of someone who is not awakened by babies at six in the morning. She is hanging on to my husband's every word as if he were Warren Beatty, only smarter, and he is hanging on to her every word as if she were Simone de Beauvoir, only better-looking, and I am beginning to feel like Othello in *Othello*.

Yes, I admit it, I'm jealous, which I know is considered an unwholesome, unattractive, and immature emotion. My only consolation for having such an unwholesome, unattractive, and immature emotion is the suspicion—no, the certainty!—that every wife, from time to time, feels jealous too.

And why not? Jealousy isn't reserved for those cataclysmic moments when a husband packs his electric toothbrush and runs off with the lady next door. It is ready to spring at far, far less provocation—a lingering glance at a swaying bell-bottomed bottom, an extended conversation with that long-haired 19-year-old, or even an undue enthusiasm for the lady next door's views on water pollution. In fact, we can become jealous of our husband's family, his business partner, his best friend, his psychiatrist, or his entire bowling team if we feel he is seeking or finding in them something that he isn't getting from us.

Other women, however, tend to make us more jealous than bowling teams. What many of us worry about, I suppose, after we've been married for a few years, is that we no longer constantly dazzle and delight the man we've married. He's seen us at breakfast wearing the terry-cloth robe with the torn sleeve, a smudge of last night's mascara under our eyes. He's seen us with bellyaches and without the padded bra, shaving our legs and wearing rollers and screaming at the plumber.

He may guess that other women also snore, snarl, and sometimes forget to rinse out their stockings, but when he looks at his lawfully wedded wife he doesn't have to guess —he knows. He knows, we know he knows, and so if an attractive, *unknown* woman smiles at him (or he at her) across a crowded room and they eventually wind up on the same couch nibbling on the same hors d'oeuvre, we feel a twinge of jealousy.

If the appeal of another woman worries us, it's not only because she is unknown to our husband in that special, married sense of torn terry-cloth robes, but also because he is unknown to her. Which means that when he talks about his business trip to Denver (he's told you about it three times) she glows with interest, and when he complains about his bad back (you warned him not to pick up that heavy box) she pouts with sympathy, and when he tells her that hilarious story about the poker game (he lost $50 and you really don't see what's so funny) she howls with appreciative laughter.

Is she putting him on? Does she mean it? Can she actually want to know why he is thinking of buying a Ford instead of a Chevy—or is it the other way around—next year?

Yes, she probably does want to know. She hasn't heard it all before, and if this nice-looking man wants to confide to her his innermost thoughts on automotive design, she'll be happy to listen. Wives listen too—of course they do—but rarely with the flattering concentration (and glows and pouts and howls of laughter) that other women muster without effort. Watching a husband's ego expand under this treatment, watching the obvious pleasure he derives from this brief (we hope) encounter, we may very well be stabbed by jealousy.

Another distressing effect of the other woman is her talent for evoking in our thoroughly familiar mates new aspects, hidden depths, and secret yearnings. A married lady can pick up some astounding items of information about her husband simply by observing him tête-à-tête with another female. For instance . . .

Husband to philosophy major home from fashionable

women's college for the holidays: "Yes, I've often thought that Nietzsche had a profound grasp of the human condition." Is that what he's often thought? How come he never mentioned it to me?

Husband to dazzlingly chic career woman: "There's no question that a life without children can be freer, more exciting." This is the man who has been trying to talk me into a fourth baby for the last two years?

Husband to sun-tanned athlete with sprinkling of freckles across her adorable nose: "I've been dying to try the surfing at Waikiki." He has, has he? First of all, he doesn't know which end of a surfboard is up. Second of all, salt water makes him itch. And third of all, we'd probably have to give him mouth-to-mouth resuscitation if he ever got anywhere near the Perfect Wave.

Many of my friends have discovered for the first time, thanks to a little discreet surveillance, that their husbands can quote entire verses of Catullus, or yearn to chuck their jobs and become veterinarians, or wish they had gone to Harvard, or wish they hadn't gone to Harvard, or are thinking seriously of converting to Zen. They've also discovered that, spurred onward by an unwifely smile, a husband can suddenly master the art of lighting a lady's cigarette and finding her pocketbook and even listening to every word *she* says. And while he is feeling charmed, charming, soulful, profound, witty, gallant, and titillated, we are feeling—yes—we are feeling jealous.

Other women, alas, are not only encountered at parties, where a wife can at least study the competition in action, spill a drink on her dress, interrupt prolonged conversations, develop a headache so she can demand to be taken home, and, once at home, attempt to bring a husband to his senses by saying, "Since when have you been reading Nietzsche?"

No, other women, alas, are everywhere. They are secretaries and waitresses and women executives and even, in our case, a very pretty lady eye doctor. They are, if a husband has some sort of service job, his customers, his clients, or his patients. They are, if a husband travels, TWA stewardesses, San Francisco go-go dancers, old flames in Minneapolis, new models in Detroit. And they are possible temptations—one and all.

I don't mean to say that we spend all our waking moments fearing that our husbands may fall into the arms of another woman. But there are many circumstances—external and internal, real and imagined, ultimately innocent or ultimately leading to disaster—that can give a wife a first-class case of jealousy.

I remember the time my husband received a bill for two from a hotel in Pennsylvania and I had never been there.

I remember the time I found the key to a local motel tucked into a corner of his dresser drawer.

I remember the time I was visiting in New York and phoned home at eight in the morning to say hi ("Just tell him his wife is calling," I told the operator) and a sweet female voice answered the phone. ("Should I still say his wife is calling?" the operator asked me.)

I needn't bother explaining what passed through my mind before I learned, incontrovertibly, that the hotel was where he had taken our oldest boy skiing, the motel key had been left behind by an out-of-town friend, and the lady on the other end of the phone was a baby-sitter brought in to get the kids off to school so my husband could attend an unexpected early meeting.

Family fights always seem to leave me particularly vulnerable to jealousy. Last month, for instance, after one of our little battles about child rearing ("Don't you ever tell that kid no?" . . . "*You* tell him no; you're the sadist in the family") we went to a PTA meeting where we met Nick's third-grade teacher. I think my husband said the weather was turning cold and the teacher said yes, it sure was, but that was enough for me. I could see that they understood each other, had total rapport, would never disagree about how to raise a child or about anything else, obviously could have a rich, full life together if only I weren't standing in their way . . . and on I went, stopping just short of where they were weeping quietly over my grave.

Whenever we're feeling low on self-esteem, chances are we can reach new heights of jealousy without much effort. If I'm feeling dowdy, I become extremely uneasy about my husband's young and gorgeous research assistants. (My husband never has old and ugly research assistants.) If I'm feeling stupid, I don't like to see him in the vicinity of a lady Ph.D. in political science. If I'm feeling very stick-in-the-mud unadventurous about life I hate having him spend any time with one of those dashing, daring females who are always doing things like diving out of airplanes in parachutes.

There are lots of wives—and I confess I'm among them—who have jealousy problems because they are persuaded that they have married a superior male, a man so marvelous that every woman must surely covet him. Thus anyone who laughs at his jokes, dances with him, asks for a lift home, or wants to discuss something personal with him at lunch becomes a potential home wrecker.

The point is, we don't have to be married to a certified love object like Paul Newman the actor to be troubled by the possible encroachment of another woman. Our husband can be Paul Newman the optometrist, but if we find him irresistible, we're likely to assume that everyone else does too.

Then there are women who are jealous of their husband not because they think he's so marvelous but because they think he's unduly susceptible to feminine wiles. To put it bluntly, they consider their man a pushover, an easy mark for any woman who so much as sits next to him on the bus. Still other wives regard their husband as a pushover for certain types, for women with special characteristics they know their man really digs. I, for example, don't like Milton getting cozy with ladies who look like Leslie Caron. My friend Elizabeth worries about women with a brilliant grasp of the urban crisis.

Well, what is it, exactly, that we are jealous about? Do we really think that within minutes after our man meets another woman they will be locked in someone's executive suite and the next day we'll get a call from the lawyer offering us a generous settlement and we keep the children? Do we think they are going to go to bed and begin a serious affair? Do we think they are going to go to bed and begin a casual affair—whatever *that* is?

I suspect that many of us, at some time, have every one of those dismal thoughts, but I also suspect that these thoughts are not what common, everyday jealousy is all about. I think the everyday kind of jealousy has less to do with a fear of overt sexual betrayal than it does with a fear of intimacy that excludes us.

If a good marriage means sharing most of life's experiences together and finding most of our satisfactions in each other—and I believe it does—then a wife may very well feel threatened when her husband seems to be sharing experiences and finding gratifications elsewhere. Although we're not unrealistic enough to believe that we are our husband's entire universe, and, I hope, not foolish enough to want to be, we sometimes see his pursuit of outside satisfactions as a rejection, an abandonment, a betrayal, of us.

I imagine that's why we can be jealous of phone calls to his mother or hikes with his best friend. (What is he telling her that he doesn't tell me? What is he discussing with him that he doesn't think I'm smart enough to understand?) And if his intimacy with these other people can make us jealous, then how very, very jealous we can become when we believe that another woman, however briefly, is making him feel something—something sweet or romantic or exciting or tender—that maybe we haven't made him feel in a long time.

In any case, it often doesn't seem to matter whether our husbands are having assignations with other women, or merely soliciting their opinion on hoof-and-mouth disease. When we are jealous, reason flees, and we do all those desperate and sometimes funny things that people tend to do when they are feeling angry and hurt.

The stony-silence technique is a great favorite among jealous wives because it succeeds in punishing the man while maintaining the dignity of the woman.

Maybe while he was out of town some lady called the house a couple of times, or a letter, pale violet and smelling of perfume, arrived in the mail. Now, you're certainly not going to humiliate yourself by asking who these women are. No, indeed. You wouldn't think of demeaning yourself by bringing up the subject. In fact, you don't particularly feel like bringing up any subject right now. So you walk around the house with your lips sealed, except for occasional monosyllabic replies.

There are others who prefer the rational discussion which, unfortunately, is rarely as rational as it pretends to be. My friend Connie, for instance, says that whenever jealousy strikes she sits down with her husband and urges him to tell all, on the grounds that she is a sensible, realistic woman who can deal intelligently with the truth, whatever it is. "And if he ever tells me that he's having an affair," Connie adds, "I'm going to grab a butcher knife and stab him right through the heart."

Sarcasm as a device for handling jealousy has the advantage of allowing a woman to simultaneously let off steam and demonstrate her devastating wit. "All right, Fred Astaire, time to go home," you may say to a husband who has been twirling around the dance floor all night with everyone but you. (You may say that, but surely there *must* be something cleverer to say.) I like sarcasm a lot, but when I'm jealous I'm usually too outraged to practice it. I do much better with more direct commentary, like Lecher! Sex maniac! Humbert Humbert!

For the jealous wife it is sometimes only a short step from such violent verbal assault to physical violence, and I'll have to admit that I do, on occasion, cross that line. Like a lot of women I may begin with indirect action—telephone slamming, or door banging—and later move on to the real thing. To date I have thrown two avocado green earthenware plates, one avocado, many books and shoes, and once—and this is direct proof of the evils of watching old movies on TV—a custard pie. I don't personally know any wives who, in a jealous rage, have shot or poisoned their possibly faithless husbands, but I am acquainted with several scratchers and one ankle-kicker.

Some women, rather than resort to wordlessness, words, or even a good kick in the ankle, express their jealousy by a relentless supervision of their husband's activities. These are the ladies who try to make sure his dentist's appointments are on Thursdays, when the cuddly, redheaded nurse is off duty and the graying-grandmother nurse is on. These are the ladies who, often with admirable skill and discretion, obtain from him a minute-by-minute report of what happened between 5:30, when he left the office, and 7:05, when he arrived home. These are also the ladies who haven't a qualm in the world about breaking up a lifelong friendship if the particular lifelong friend happens to be a footloose bachelor or an unnecessarily attractive divorcée.

It's true that I too have dropped a couple of young lovelies from our guest list, but I really don't have the time to play private eye to my husband. I prefer occupying my spare moments with self-improvement projects, on the theory that an excellent way to deal with jealousy is to attempt to become intriguingly attractive and versatile. Since we've been married I have tried to become intriguing through guitar lessons, French lessons, abstract painting, an English literature course, and—Lord help me—modern dance. Unfortunately, Milton threatened to move to a hotel if I continued with the guitar, and he finished my painting career a few years ago when he hung one of my masterpieces in the basement next to the boiler. Most of my other projects, I fear, are destined to meet a similar fate.

Anyway, whatever success we may achieve at becoming a whole new person, or even several different new people, I'm afraid we are still instantly recognizable to our mate as that same old wife in the torn terry-cloth robe. Our sad conclusion must be that we can be another woman only to another man, which is the kind of reasoning that can lead to the most dangerous and frustrating game a jealous married lady can play—trying to make her husband jealous too.

One good friend of mine, married to an intense Mediterranean type, grew unhappy about the amount of overtime he was putting in at the office, assisted by a very sexy secretary. "Oh, Michael," she told him one evening, in her most unconvincingly casual voice, "I met this actor while I was out walking the dog and I think he's going to come over Wednesday afternoon to discuss Saint Bernards." Michael, she told me, didn't bother exploring the pros and cons. Instead, he marched straight over to where she stood and gave her a resounding smack in the face, a smack that has permanently discouraged her from trying this particular gambit again.

The problem with trying to make a husband jealous is that he may wind up far angrier than we've ever bargained for. An even bigger problem, however, is that he will probably refuse—despite our determined provocation—to show the remotest signs of jealousy.

I'm afraid I've failed at the get-him-jealous game. Whenever I've played it, by making comments like "If you don't want to see that movie tonight, maybe I'll go with Andy," or, "Seth says I'd look terrific if I cut my hair short," I inevitably draw a most unsatisfying reply. "Do whatever you want," my husband always tells me. Which always leaves me doing nothing at all.

For the most part, women appear more prone to jealousy than men, and I've been trying to figure out why. Maybe it's because it is almost impossible for wives to contemplate squeezing in a rendezvous between the school play and the grocery shopping, and our husbands know this very well. Or maybe my friend from the Women's Liberation movement has the answer. "Women are more jealous," she told me scornfully, "because they're convinced of their own inferiority. They think that men do them a tremendous favor merely by staying married."

There's probably truth in that somewhere, but I'm afraid it will not alter the way I behave. I'm going to continue standing around at cocktail parties fretting over fresh-faced 19-year-olds and I'm planning to make a terrible scene if I ever find pink lipstick (mine is beige) on my husband's collar. But on those days when I happen to be feeling mature and secure I'm also going to admit that a man who wasn't attractive to other women, a man who wasn't alive enough to enjoy other women, a man who was incapable of making me jealous, would never be the kind of man I'd love.

VIII

Sex and the Married Housewife

❧❦❧

Just as there are other women in Milton's life, so are there other men in mine. There's the plumber, the electrician, the exterminator, the milkman, and the fellow I call when the kids drop a ball down the downspout.

It's true that I have an intense involvement with all of them, but nothing that you would ever describe as sexy. And as far as most of the other males I encounter, what they always want to do is—not seduce me—but show me the latest snapshots of their kids.

No, I'm not the kind who drives men drunk with desire. And yet, even into the life of a married lady with a varicose vein, declining muscle tone, and the beginnings of upper-eyelid droop, an interested male will occasionally wander.

So maybe he isn't exactly drunk with desire. But he's certainly thirsty.

I've always wished I could handle such occasions with wit and grace and charm and flair and style. But instead . . .

It's one in the morning at Jackie Carlin's anniversary party, and I am dancing with Jackie's husband's old fraternity brother, a dashing bachelor who is breathing heavily into my inner ear and running his manicured fingers through my hairpiece. The lights are low, the music slow and dreamy, and while I—one of the inept dancers of this world—am trying to follow his tricky little dance steps, he is pressing my basic black Banlon into his chest.

"Are you thinking what I'm thinking?" he sighs, massaging my shoulder blades.

I decide not to answer that question. I decide not to answer it because what I'm thinking is that I told the sitter we'd be home no later than 12, and that I didn't buy any milk for the children's breakfast. I am also wondering how in the world I'm going to get Anthony to his judo lesson since Milton wants to bring in the car for a tune-up. Furthermore, I'm trying to decide whether to risk washing the shower curtain by machine or . . .

"Your perfume," he whispers, "is driving me wild. What is it?"

"Well," I explain, "it isn't really perfume that you're smelling. It's this antidandruff stuff I use—called Dri-Stop."

"Adorable," he murmurs, kissing the outer corner of my eye. "And so are you."

"That's very kind of you," I say, missing a beat and tripping over his boot. "Excuse me."

His hands leave my back and start moving slowly southward. "A beautiful woman," he says with infinite tenderness, "never has to ask to be excused."

This kind of kills the conversation for a while, and I go back to trying not to trip. His hands are still heading south.

"I'm glad you don't wear a girdle," he tells me approvingly, having just established that fact to his satisfaction.

I try to reply in a very businesslike manner. "You could have *asked* me if I wore one," I say. "You didn't have to bother doing research."

He chuckles. "Your sense of humor," he tells me, "is delicious. And so," he adds, biting my neck, "are you."

I imagine explaining teeth marks to my husband, which makes me miss a beat and trip again. He draws me closer and whispers, with sudden urgency, "I want to know everything about you. Meet me for lunch Monday."

His grip is tight and I'm having trouble breathing. "Mondays are out," I gasp. "I always defrost the refrigerator Mondays."

He spins me around once or twice and murmurs, "Tuesday then?"

I shake my head. "Impossible," I say. "What with my root canal and the gingivitis, I'm booked up every Tuesday with the dentist."

"Wednesday," he hisses, pressing his lips to my palm.

"My marketing day," I explain. "Plus I help at the library."

"And Thursday?" he asks, but his voice is growing colder.

"That's the changing-the-sheets-and-getting-my-hair-done day."

There's a very long silence.

I am planning to tell him that Fridays I drive the car pool and like to do my mending for the week. But he never asks. And since he also stops with the patting and kissing and biting, I am left with the definite impression that, rather than wanting to know everything about me, he already knows too much.

"Would you like a drink?" I ask him, being friendly, as he steers me—rather sternly—off the floor.

"No," he replies and leads me back to my husband. "I was feeling thirsty earlier this evening. But I'm sure not feeling thirsty anymore."

You see what I mean about wit and grace and flair. But how do you tell a man a sensuous no? I'd love to have left him thinking sad thoughts like "To think she will never be mine." But the thought that he's left with, I fear, is, "I'm sorry I asked."

It was once explained to me that the reason other men don't ask more often is that MARRIED is written in large red letters on my brow. "You seem as available for an illicit affair," I was told, "as Mary Poppins."

But there are other kinds of affairs—I guess they're called licit—in which all is known and forgiven in advance. You needn't be sneaky. You needn't feel guilty. All you need do is . . . swap.

In other words, the other man in my life could be somebody's husband, if I were willing to give that somebody mine. Or so my friend Grace recently pointed out. . . .

"I just finished reading this article on swapping," she said, as we sat around drinking coffee in her kitchen. "And I'll tell you something—it made a lot of sense."

I choked on a sip and quickly put down my cup. Already I didn't like the conversation.

"You never know," she continued, quite in earnest. "Maybe we're missing a major human experience. Maybe we're allowing life to pass us by."

The subject was making me very, very nervous. "Why don't we talk about floor wax," I suggested.

(78)

"No," Grace said. "I'm serious. For the open-minded, self-assured individual, swapping could add an exciting new dimension to marriage."

"But I'm close-minded, and I'm insecure, and my marriage already has more dimensions than I can handle," I said. "Let's discuss detergents."

"It could teach us to be more generous, more giving," said Grace.

"Milton gave at the office," I told her. "Let's compare cleansers."

Grace put her hand on my shoulder. "You know what I think," she said. "I think you're trying to deny your secret, suppressed, tumultuous, passionate yearnings. It just so happens that I've seen you look at my Ronnie, and I know that somewhere, deep inside, you want him."

"Your *Ronnie!*" I screeched. "You've got to be kidding! Your Ronnie has tufts of hair growing in his ears. He wears a diamond pinky ring, for God's sake. I could never in a million years be attracted to a hairy-eared man with a pinky ring."

I guess I hurt Grace's feelings. "Don't think your Milton is such a bargain either," she snapped back at me vengefully. "His feet are enormous. I've always found men with big feet exceedingly gross."

"You have some nerve talking about gross," I said, "when your Ronnie, only a week ago, showed his appendix scar in mixed company."

"Some men," sniffed Grace, "aren't ashamed of their bodies."

"Some men," I sniffed back, "ought to be."

We glared at each other silently for several minutes. Then I said, "Come on, Grace, this is ridiculous. You keep your Ronnie. I'll keep my Milton. And now, could we please talk about whether Top Job is better than Lestoil?"

"You're refusing," said Grace, "to face what you really feel in your heart of hearts."

"But what I really feel in my heart of hearts," I told her, "is that I'm a happily married woman who loves her husband and doesn't want anyone else's."

Grace frowned. "It's unwholesome attitudes like yours," she said, "that are responsible for the high divorce rate in this country."

I tried to change the subject by asking Grace if she'd found Palmolive more satisfactory than Colgate, but she wouldn't answer. Instead, she sat staring dreamily out the kitchen window.

"I'll bet," she said to me after a couple of moments, "that there are swappers all around us, only we don't know it."

"You're crazy, Grace," I said. "That article has affected your mind."

"Don't be so naïve," she answered. "Appearances can be very deceiving. Why, there was a photograph of some swappers in the newspaper who looked exactly like Tina and Jerry Blumberg."

"It just so happens," I said, "that I know the Blumbergs rather well, and let me tell you something—they are the kind of people who think Pat and Richard Nixon are oversexed."

"Those are the kind to watch," Grace said. "And the Dorsens, too."

"Oh, stop it!" I groaned. "Mr. Dorsen is 78 years old, and he's confined to a wheelchair besides."

"Lust will out," said Grace serenely.

I decided that the time had come to make one thing perfectly clear. "I'm not quite sure what you're driving at, Grace," I said, "but if this is one of those Bob and Alice and Carol and Ted proposals, I want you to know that I'm only interested in talking toilet tissues."

Grace pretended she hadn't heard me. "Our king-sized water bed is being delivered today," she said. "Why don't you and Milton come take a look at it this evening?"

Quick as a flash I replied, "Only if you'll let us bring the kids."

"Of course," said Grace—and a note of bitterness crept into her voice. "But only if you'll let us tell you why we would rather use Ajax than Bab-o."

I guess it's too bad, in a way, that I lack a spirit of sexual adventure. But I really don't have the time for clandestine rendezvous and as far as swapping goes, suppose he decided that Grace was better than me?

Still, there's no question that I and most of the wives I know are delighted to stir up the interest of other men. We're delighted, however, not because we want them to take us to bed, but because our charms are confirmed by the fact that they want to.

Furthermore, as my cousin Ruthie recently demonstrated, there is nothing like another man's attentions to help a husband rediscover his wife. . . .

It seems that Leon, my cousin Ruthie's husband, was neglecting her—so she decided to take serious steps.

"Listen, I'm not talking about anything drastic," she assured me, when she phoned last week from Queens. "I just want that rotten Leon to wake up and realize that I'm still a sought-after, lust-inspiring woman."

Well, what could I say? My cousin Ruthie is sweet. She's intelligent. She's a swell cook. She's even rather pretty, in a round and cozy den-mother way. But lust-inspiring? If Shirley Booth is lust-inspiring, so's my cousin Ruthie, if you know what I mean.

Anyway, yesterday I got another call from Queens. "I

just bought a topless jump suit," said Ruthie, all excited. "And false eyelashes. And a perfume called Rape that the salesgirl swore was very lust-inspiring."

"That's nice," I told Ruthie. "What do you have in mind?"

What she had in mind, Ruthie said, was to wear all her purchases that very night, when the Kew Gardens Bridge Club met at her house. "I figure," she said, "that the husbands will go wild. And when that rotten Leon sees their passion rising, he'll look at me with new eyes."

"That's some plan," I said, not with much conviction. "Be sure to call tomorrow and let me know how it turns out."

She just finished letting me know.

The evening, it seems, started out very unpromising. Ruthie puts on the whole ensemble—the jump suit, the lashes, the Rape—and it's like she's in her ninth month. No response.

Okay, she tells herself, they're concentrating on the card game. But later, when she's serving the coffee and cheese-cake and still no response, she gets a little discouraged.

Finally, she's clearing the table and walking into the kitchen, when who should follow her but Leon's friend Harold.

"Shhh," he whispers, kicking the door shut. "I don't want my wife to hear."

She tells him she understands perfectly.

"I'm sorry," he says. "I know it's a sneaky thing to do."

"Harold, darling," she answers. "I understand perfectly."

He pats her on the arm. "You're a very understanding woman," he says. He sighs and pats her arm again.

And then, you won't believe this, he reaches behind her —at this point, mind you, she's ready to slap his hand—cuts himself an enormous slice of cheesecake, and jams it into his mouth.

(82)

"Harold!" she screams. "What are you doing?"

"Oh, God," he moans. "Oh, God. It's so fantastic." He cuts another piece.

"Harold," she tells him, "this is absolutely disgusting."

He swallows the second piece whole. "She won't let me eat it," he says, wiping his mouth with the back of his wrist. "She says it's bad for my cholesterol. Ruthie, I love cheesecake more than life itself, and my wife won't let me eat it."

Finally he pulls himself together and they go back to the living room. Harold's wife looks at them and says, "Ho, ho, what have you two been doing?"

Harold gives Ruthie a wink—you know, very conspiratorial—and says, "We'll never tell."

That's when Leon makes his fatal mistake. "What," he says with a laugh, "could there be to tell?"

At this point, Ruthie admitted, she went crazy. She looks at Leon very coldly and says, "If you want to know, wise guy, I was out there fighting off your dear friend Harold, who was propositioning me and other dirty things. He says he can't keep his hands off me. He says I'm very lust-inspiring. Think about *that*."

Then she gives Harold this conspiratorial wink, and as Ruthie points out, "What is the poor man going to do? Can he call me a liar? Can he confess to his wife about the cheesecake? Of course not. Better he should claim that someone spiked his drink with LSD and he lost his head."

Well, she goes up to bed, and a few minutes later up comes Leon.

"All of a sudden," he says to Ruthie, "I'm looking at you with new eyes."

"Leon, darling," she says, "I understand perfectly."

It was obviously a very mutual understanding, because this weekend, Ruthie told me, Leon is taking her to the Virgin Islands for a second honeymoon.

"I won't be needing the topless jump suit anymore," she

said before she hung up. "Why don't I send it down to you?"

"Please, Ruthie," I told her, "forget the jump suit. Just send me down that recipe for cheesecake."

IX

Such Good Friends

In addition to Other Women and Other Men, a married life is full of many friends.

We laugh with them when they're happy.

We hold their hand when they're sad.

We lend them our car, or a sympathetic ear.

We feed their cats and water their plants and pick them up at the airport, and we dearly love and cherish them—most of the time.

The rest of the time, however, certain problems may arise.

For instance, when we're making out our will.

For although my husband and I are rather stable types, we've already changed our will five different times. Our concern hasn't been with who gets the stocks, the Old Masters, the fabled Viorstian diamond, the trust funds, the yacht. Our only concern has been which of our friends get the kids.

Now since I'm the kind of person who sees death lurking around every corner, I've been persuaded that, at almost any moment, Milton and I could depart this world together, the victims of snipers or earthquakes or bolts from the blue. I've decided therefore that it's very important to select the proper guardians for our potentially orphaned young sons—some loving, dependable, happily married couple who not only adore the children, but also share our hopes, our values, our aspirations, our magazine subscriptions, and, if possible, our swim club.

Which is precisely why we've revised our will five times.

Our first effort at willing the children to someone was back in 1963, when we selected Arnold and Emily, the happiest couple we knew. She ironed his shirts, and he dropped her off at the beauty parlor, and she fixed him homemade muffins for breakfast, and he fixed her champagne cocktails for dinner, and she always said how witty and brilliant he was, and he always said how attractive and charming she was.

In 1963 they were very happy.

In 1964, however, Arnold started to dally with a go-go dancer, after which Emily started to dally with a urologist, after which they decided to get a divorce, making us suspect that they probably weren't the happiest couple we knew. We unhesitatingly cut them out of our will, replacing them with Mike and Shirley, who, as they'd often told us, adored our boys.

Unfortunately we made the mistake of *first* establishing Mike and Shirl as our kids' legal guardians and *then* notifying them of the great honor we had conferred upon them.

They weren't, it turned out, anywhere near as honored as we thought they'd be.

"They're nice kids to visit," said Shirl, rather coldly, "but I wouldn't want them to live here."

"Don't worry," Mike assured her, "they won't. In fact, if we're not removed from that will by noon tomorrow, we're suing."

We don't see Mike and Shirley anymore.

We ran into exactly the opposite situation with guardians number three.

The Fishers were a lovely couple, the kind who, if Milton and I were driving in a car and it plunged off an icy bridge into the river, would make us feel downright serene about the whole thing. But a few months after we'd installed them in our will, they suggested that we make the arrangement reciprocal—that is, that we agree to become the guardians of their loathsome, creepy kids.

Our refusal was terribly suave and terribly tactful. "We couldn't," we told them. "We really don't deserve it." Nevertheless, the friendship began to cool soon thereafter, and we figured we'd better change the will again.

The fourth set of guardians were harder to find, but I surely thought Jessie and Bob were the perfect choice. They were charter members of our swim club as well as early supporters of peace, ecology, sideburns, and Ralph Nader. Who, if Milton and I got trapped in a burning building, could better inculcate our kids with our cherished ideals?

But the balloon burst last February, when we went to see a revival of *Casablanca*. We loved it, and they hated it, and we hated them for hating it, and they hated us for loving it. Later that night, when Milton and I were in bed, we asked each other if we could allow our boys to be raised by people who didn't even want Sam to play it again. Next morning we were back at the lawyer's office.

Finally, last week, after a good deal of soul-searching, we've managed to pick out guardians number five.

I'm worried about the way Ted smiles at his secretary, but I think the marriage will probably endure. And Milton thought Rhoda was a little snappish when Alexander put his foot through their TV screen, but he thinks she'll probably be kind. We've even agreed to become the guardians of *their* children, a commitment which involves two boys, three gerbils, a cat, a dog, and a small but hostile lizard.

We don't want to know their opinion of *Casablanca*.

We're hoping we've finally settled the guardian question. We're hoping we'll never revise our will again.

The lawyer's bills are getting quite expensive.

The children are getting quite confused.

And furthermore, we're running out of friends.

No, there's nothing like making a will to make you reassess your friends.

Unless it's making a guest list for dinner next Friday.

"Okay," I said to Milton the other evening. "Which three couples should we invite?"

"Joe and Martha. Roger and Jean. Artie and Louise," says Milton, right off the bat. "We owe each of them about 20 invitations."

"If you're trying to imply," I say, "that I never take the trouble to entertain, I'm walking out of the living room this minute. And besides—that's an impossible combination."

"What do you mean impossible?"

"In the first place, Jean and Martha aren't speaking ever since Martha swiped Jean's baby-sitter. And Joe is still a violent hawk, while Louise is a violent Another Mother for Peace."

(*88*)

"All right. Then what about Jean and Roger, and Rick and Nancy, and Matt and René?"

"Oh, no. Not Rick and Nancy. If I have to hear his vasectomy story one more time I'm going to scream."

"And Matt and René?"

"But then we'd have to invite someone important."

"You mean like my Uncle Irv with the seven shoe stores?"

"No. I mean like at least a Supreme Court Justice. Or an Academy Award-winning director. Or a thrice-divorced noted horsewoman heiress. Matt and René would find our real friends boring."

"Then how come they don't find *us* boring?"

"Honey, they *do* find us boring. But who do you think fills in for René on her car pool days, when she's all tied up with those heiresses and directors?"

"I guess that only leaves us Jean and Roger."

"Not *us*, darling. *You*. I remember the last time Jean came over for dinner. By the time she got finished kissing you hello, your shirt was unbuttoned all the way down to your belly button."

"Ah, yes. Right. It all comes back to me now. That Jeannie gives a hell of a hello kiss."

"Stop salivating and think of the names of six people."

"Would you want to try Lois and Freddie with Pete and Gloria and Betsy and Dick?"

"Freddie *and* Pete? We can't have two orthodontists, for heaven's sake."

"But if we just have one orthodontist, who's going to talk to him?"

"You've got something there. Maybe we shouldn't have any."

"Then we're scratching them all, except for Betsy and Dick?"

"You aren't going to be happy with Betsy and Dick. They are now militant vegetarians, and every time you chew on a piece of lamb they remind you that once it scampered gaily o'er hill and dale. Believe me, that's a real appetite killer."

"I see what you mean. But tell me, do we know anyone else?"

"Of course we do, silly. The Goldens, the Colemans, and the Rumsens. They'll be crazy about each other."

"I hate to be negative, dear, but I honestly don't think I can sit down to dinner with a Mitzi, a Fritzi, and a Bitsie, all at once."

"But don't you think that could make for a fun evening?"

"Only if Bitsie does her bird imitations. Come on, Judy, think of some other names."

"Well then, why don't we invite some intellectuals. You know, deep-thinking types, like the Walters, the Palmers, and the Sidemans."

"Herbie Palmer a deep-thinking type? Don't make me laugh. Look, he's a perfectly lovely fellow, but *The Fountainhead* is still his favorite book."

"I realize that. As a matter of fact, we had a very profound discussion of that book a couple of weeks ago, and maybe he sees things in it that you just don't."

"I am not spending an evening discussing *The Fountainhead* with Herbie Palmer, and that's that. I am also not having my dreams analyzed by Ken Walters. As for Mortimer Sideman, don't flatter yourself that he's interested in your mind. When he says Newtonian physics, baby, that's his crafty way of making a pass."

"Okay. I quit. I give up. Do you want us to have this dinner party or don't you?"

"Dinner for six? I think we'd better forget it. At the rate we're going, we'll barely make tea for two."

Still, despite these little problems with guest lists and wills, most of the time we're devoted to our friends. We'll join with them to celebrate their wedding anniversaries— and help them when their marriages collapse.

Yes, every time a couple we know starts talking about divorce, the first thing I ask is, Can this marriage be saved?

The only proper response, of course, is None of your business, but I'm incapable of thinking along such lines. "Come over tonight, the two of you," I urge the divorcing duo, "before you do anything rash."

The concept behind this invitation is psychologically sound, according to the psych course I took in college. Give two unhappy people the opportunity to fully express their angers and resentments and, with a little help from their friends, they'll be able to see how much they really love each other.

I still say it's a terrific concept, but in more than a decade of free marriage counseling, I've yet to effect a single reconciliation. Indeed, there have been evenings when these self-expression sessions have threatened the equilibrium of my own happy home.

Take the other night, with Milton and me and Alma and Sheldon.

Milton: Alma, you look great. That dress is a real knockout.

Sheldon: It should be—I paid a small fortune for it.

Alma: With Sheldon, if it's over $10.95 it's a small fortune.

Milton: Well, I still say you look lovely, and not a day older than when we first met.

Sheldon: Which was when, last week?

Me: Shelly, you always did have a swell sense of humor.

Alma: He sure does. Last March, when I slipped on the ice and almost got hit by a car, I thought he'd die laughing.

Sheldon: This is a woman who can't walk from the living room to the bathroom without almost getting hit by a car. To hear Alma tell it, she's dodged death more times than a World War I flying ace.

Alma: I should only get the kind of sympathy that flying aces get. Sheldon is incapable—and I mean *incapable*—of even a drop of pity.

Me: But Alma, why not accept the fact that men are, by nature, very self-centered people? That's something I learned long, long ago, and let me tell you—it's helped keep our marriage going.

Milton: What did she say that she learned long, long ago?

Sheldon: That you're a selfish s. o. b. who wouldn't lift a finger in her behalf.

Milton: I'm not even going to comment on that, considering that I've given her back rubs and made her tea with honey for her cough I couldn't begin to count how many times.

Me: Don't worry—he's counted the times. He's probably got them written down in a book somewhere.

Alma: Could I have just a teensy bit more of the Rémy Martin? I have to admit Milton certainly knows his cognacs. And that concerto on the stereo is sublime.

Sheldon: Listen to her with the cognacs and concertos. For 13 years she's been drinking malteds and listening to Mantovani, but suddenly I'm married to an aesthete.

Alma: Sheldon is essentially very insecure with cultivated people. He'd like to keep everyone down—down at *his* level.

Me: I think it's wonderful that you two understand each other so well. I mean, isn't that the *sine qua non* of any healthy relationship?

Milton: You're not pronouncing that right. Will you do me a favor and stick to the English language?

Me: Will you do me a favor and stop trying to humiliate me in public?

Alma: I've been saying that to Shelly since we've been married, but it's hopeless. He's got a streak of cruelty in him that's almost frightening.

Sheldon: Look at her, she's really frightened, isn't she?

Me: I think we're all a little frightened of our own inner feelings. It's so important to get them out in the open, don't you think?

Milton: I think you should take the glasses out to the kitchen.

Sheldon: I think the Rémy Martin is giving me heartburn.

Alma: I think I'm calling my lawyer in the morning.

I think I must be doing something wrong.

X

Such Relatives

❧❦❧

It's always sad to see a couple break up, especially when we've all been such good friends. But anything that can possibly happen to any friend of ours has already happened in spades to the folks in New Jersey.

We hear about it through the U.S. mails.

Yes, almost 12 years ago, as my husband and I slipped away from our wedding feast, a figure suddenly rushed to the door and called after us.

"Write!" cried this voice into the wind. "Write every day. Remember, darling, I'm your only mother."

Since darling's only mother is also my only mother-in-law, we've kept up a correspondence ever after. Our side of it, I'm afraid, has been rather dull. But with so many relatives—and *such* relatives—all over northern New Jersey, my mother-in-law has had more than plenty to say.

We write, for instance, that we bought a new chair for the living room.

She writes that Uncle Ben's business went into receivership.

We write that Alexander can now ride his bike.

She writes that her unmarried niece is a little bit pregnant.

We write that it looks like the lilacs are starting to bloom.

She writes that it looks like Aunt Hannah is having a breakdown.

For, operating on the theory that good news is no news and that every silver lining has a cloud, my mother-in-law has relayed to us now for lo! these many years a continuing drama of torment, pain, and suffering. Her letters testify to the fact that while lesser folks must find their pleasures in pleasure, it takes a true connoisseur to savor the joys of sorrow.

"Hi, Everybody," each of her letters begin.

"We're all fine. The chest pains only bother me at bedtime and if I don't move my shoulder I hardly notice the arthritis. It's amazing how many sleepless nights a person is able to live through, and still get up and cook and clean all day.

"I hope nobody mentioned to you about my lump, which I'm having checked by the doctor a week from today. I certainly wouldn't want you to be worrying yourself sick about it the way all my friends are.

"Dad is holding his own since the automobile accident— his fifth this year. For a man who drives as carefully as he does, he's been running into an awful lot of bad luck. But go explain that to the insurance company, which is quick to assume that whenever a person hits a parked car, it's his fault.

"Your second cousin Richie just quit medical school. He wants to be a harpsichord tuner, what else?

"His mother cried for a week, but he's still quitting.

"Then his mother went to bed with a high fever, but he's still quitting.

"Then his mother took an overdose of aspirin but he's still quitting.

"I told him he'll wind up playing the harpsichord at his mother's funeral, and his answer I'm too ashamed to repeat. Where a heart should be, that Richie has a rock.

"Judy, darling, you'd probably like to know that your father's sister is suffering from such earaches that the surgeon is considering amputation.

"Also, her daughter Googie delivered a beautiful baby after being in labor 60 hideous hours.

"Also, if you'll put the rest of Nicky's pants in the mail, I'll gladly shorten them. Call me old-fashioned, but when I see my grandson tripping over his cuffs, and about to get at least a multiple fracture, it hurts me.

"Your Aunt Flo is in a very severe depression, having just been defeated for the presidency of the Mah-Jongg club. It was most unexpected.

"Here, after all, is one of those rare human beings who everyone loves and needs and trusts and turns to. She has so many friends and so many confidantes, she makes Golda Meir look like a social outcast. Strangers on the street—I can personally testify—rush over to pour in her ear their most intimate longings.

"I might also say that last year, when Flo's cyst was removed, she received, from people all over the world and New Jersey, 29 house plants, 36 floral arrangements, and 548 cards that said Get Well.

"Her nurses adored her.

"What's more, in addition to *that*, the butcher always saves her the leanest pot roasts; and the fish man always gives her the fresh, not the frozen; and the man at the bake shop, famous for palming off cake that is one day old, always makes certain that Flo's cake just came from the oven.

"You'll have to admit that's a very popular person.

"So now please go explain how Sandra Hyman, who, in her entire medical history, never received a total of 29 house plants, could possibly win the Mah-Jongg club election.

"We suspect foul play.

"Marlene, Sonia's daughter, is talking of leaving her husband, on the grounds that he drinks too much and runs around. He also recently gave her a punch in the mouth for cooking his three-minute eggs for only two minutes.

"Sonia keeps trying to tell her that nobody's perfect, and that happiness is in the eye of the beholder, and who cares about happiness as long as you have your health. But Marlene was always a very fussy girl.

"And speaking of a couple going phhhtttt, we're very concerned what's happening with Rona, who now has bright red hair and a new nose.

"When a woman who's been married for 17 years decides to dye her hair and get a nose job, I say it's to worry.

"But maybe your mother just has a dirty mind.

"The recession is hitting everyone in town. It's gotten so bad that people who used to buy High Test are now buying Regular. And if I tell you Mo's brother-in-law, Mike Herman, a multimillionaire to say the least, isn't getting his daughter's teeth straightened this year because of the cost, you know the economy is in pretty serious trouble.

"I understand that you were in Manhattan last week, but

somehow didn't find any time to phone. Believe me, I'm not reproaching you—not for a minute. But I did say to myself, That's some recession, when an only son can't spare a quarter for a call.

"Remember Elsie from around the corner? Dead.

"Remember Bernie from across the street? Dead.

"Remember Aunt Minna's parakeet? Dead.

"All the phone calls in the world won't help them now.

"My brother Harry just came back from Las Vegas, where he lost the mortgage payment, the car payment, and the second installment on Yetta's blond mink stole.

"There's only one thing to call him—a broken man.

"Yetta, however, is calling him a few other things, which I'd rather not go into right now.

"Mildred, by the way, really enjoyed her visit to your house, when she made that trip to Washington with the Sisterhood. Let me just say that I personally feel that two hours is not much time to devote to a person's aunt, though I may be mistaken.

"And let me also mention, as long as I'm mentioning, that while she very much likes a plate of tuna-fish salad, your fancy spices gave her indigestion. Judy, darling, remember—we're very plain people.

"Aunt Mildred also said that the curtains looked lovely.

"And the bedspread looked lovely.

"And the chair you bought for the living room looked lovely.

"She suggests, however, that if you'd buy the large-size Breath O'Pine disinfectant, maybe you could get rid of that terrible cat smell.

"I forgot to mention the death of Charlie my butcher. He hadn't heard from his daughter in 17 days, and a lot of people thought that a call at just the right moment might have saved him.

"A pity.

"The pictures you sent of the kids were very lovely, but I almost fainted to see how thin they looked. You notice I am not commenting on their hairstyles since you explained to me that even high government officials have children who you couldn't tell from baboons. Nevertheless, it would save me a lot of embarrassment if someone would wash their faces before you snapped.

"I understand, by the way, that when Mildred was down there, the children played with their friends the entire time and wouldn't even give her a kiss good-bye. Tell them for me that blood is thicker than water.

"Your Cousin Viv is going on one of those Swinging Singles weekends, and maybe—God willing—she'll bring herself home a man.

"It's not so easy.

"Already the poor girl has gone on nine Let's Get Acquainted cruises, and seven Schussing With Swingles ski weeks, and one of those For Mature Unmarrieds parties they advertise in all the dirty papers.

"Don't ask what goes on at those parties.

"In addition, she has contacted several Computer Dating Services with so far bad—if not insulting—results.

"Meanwhile, you could maybe keep on the lookout for some steady decent fellow down by you. Surely there must be someone in the nation's capital who would be interested in a girl with a sweet disposition—though, admittedly, not a Sophia Loren—who has had elocution lessons, dancing (both ballroom and tap), nine years of piano, four years of college, a master's in sociology, and whose father would gladly take him into his business.

"We only ask he should be of the same faith.

"Judy, darling, you'd probably like to know that your nephew Eddie was thrown out of Sunday school.

"And your nephew Paulie was found in the locker room, smoking.

(99)

"And your cousin Maurice has decided gay is good.

"I thank the Lord that when I was raising a child that kind of nonsense wasn't going on.

"You might also like to know that your father's youngest sister, who admits—and that's only *admits*—to 63, is giving serious thought to buying a motorcycle. She has not been herself since she rented her spare room to that 21-year-old law student.

"Did I tell you that Barry, who only lives a couple of miles from his mother, gives her a phone call every single day? He says, and I quote, If it makes you happy, Mother, it makes me happy.

"My son should only develop such a philosophy.

"Mel has hives.

"Sheckie has a hernia.

"Morris has ingrown toenails which is no laughing matter.

"I don't plan to tell you what Mildred said about your children's language, which she happened to hear them use when she was there.

"It's none of *her* business.

"It's none of *my* business.

"It's nobody's business but yours.

"I would only like to point out that during all those years that Milton lived at home, a four-letter word never once crossed his lips.

"Roz and Len have just redone their house, and Buckingham Palace should only look so good. What with the pine-paneled rec room with built-in bar and fish tank, the dining area with genuine Spanish tile, the sunken tub with golden swans for fixtures, and the fountain with colored waters in the yard, it is truly a vision.

"Why would a kid run away from a home like that?

"We've gotten some beautiful postcards from Uncle Normie, who, as you know, is in Europe for 14 days.

"He says London is great.

"He says Rome is fantastic.

"He says Paris is the most gorgeous place in the world.

"In view of the problems he has with his stomach and dentures, however, he thinks he might have been better off in Florida.

"I suppose you'll be proud to hear that your cousin Glen is a conscientious objector. Don't think his mother is so proud.

"Your father decided to save a couple of dollars by trying to fix the television himself. Since he is not exactly the handiest man in New Jersey, our building was plunged into darkness for 45 minutes, in the course of which Mrs. Elkin tripped in the hallway and is now suing.

"Rudy was not accepted at any of the colleges of his choice.

"I just met your cousin Arnie's new wife. It's to cry. She doesn't know how to cook; she just defrosts. She doesn't know how to mend; she just throws out. The plant we sent for a present she doesn't water. The molding over the windows she doesn't dust.

"I give it a month.

"Judy, darling, I think you might like to know that your sister—a sensitive girl—is also hurt that you never bother to phone. This, anyway, is the impression I got when I ran into her at Cookie's confirmation, which you and Milton were the only ones in the family that didn't attend.

"Your sister, by the way, was truly a vision in her yellow dress with the matching scarf and coat, but something's got to be done about that cough of hers. Be a considerate sister, darling, and make her go to an eye, ear, nose, and throat man. Blood, you should never forget, is thicker than water.

"Hy from 26th Street was mugged in the alley.

"My sister Edith's purse was snatched on the bus.

"Yesterday morning early I left the apartment and there were bloodstains on the sidewalk outside our door. I only pray they didn't come from our building.

"Well, so long for now, and be sure to keep in touch. It always gives me a lift to get your letters. Hoping you feel the same,

"Love,

"Mother."

XI

Eating Is Not the Most Important Thing in Life?

⚜

From my mother-in-law, in addition to letters, come jars full of homemade chopped liver. But my husband—her son —now has fancier menus in view. For at some point in his journey through life dear Milton—who was raised on boiled chicken and soup greens and noodle pudding—discovered, as other men have discovered religion, the joys of fine cuisine.

The trouble is that now that he's discovered them, he doesn't intend to let anyone forget.

Take the other evening, for example, when we were leaving a dinner party and Milton, who is ever the gallant guest, pecked the hostess on the cheek and observed, "You certainly always try your best, Bernice, you really do. And one of these days I think you're going to make it."

What *I* think will happen one of these days is that Bernice is going to swat my husband on the head with her tin-lined copper sauté pan, and perhaps put an end to his culinary critiques. Although he is, in most ways, a quite considerate fellow, he is a gourmet of the very worst sort —he eats and tells.

It's bad enough when he tells *me*, on the ride home, that there were insufficient shallots in the salad and an excess of gelatin in the Bavarian cream. But when he offers the hostess the full benefit of his critical powers—"I don't want to hurt your feelings, sweetie, but maybe paella just isn't your dish"—I think he goes too far.

Unfortunately there are, among our friends, probably eight or ten women with whom my husband feels so cozy and comfortable that he never hesitates to keep them informed of their cooking triumphs and debacles.

"They like it," he insists. "They're grateful that someone cares enough. And when I tell them that the sauce velouté was superb, they can be sure that I'm not simply being polite."

It's my opinion that most of these ladies would happily settle for polite. A few of them, in fact, have confessed to me that they'd love to invite us for dinner more often, but they just can't take the strain.

"After I'd prepared the duck à l'orange," one of my friends informed me about a month ago, "I decided I didn't have the nerve to serve it to Milton. Not that it was bad. It just wasn't—what does the dear fellow call it?—exquisite."

Hostesses who have the good fortune not to be intimates of my husband can feed him without the risk of public humiliation, although, as I mentioned, he'll certainly talk about them behind their backs. While other men gossip about how can Nat be married to such a nag or such a grouch or such a spendthrift, Milton always wonders how he can be married to a woman with the gall to use instant coffee.

Milton, I should point out, is the world's champion instant-coffee detector. It can be poured out of an antique silver pot into a Spode china cup and served on a crystal tray by an English-accented waiter in white gloves, but you can count on him to spot it every time. And so can I— because of the look of outrage on his face.

In the life of the gourmet, however, outrage is a rather familiar emotion, readily inspired by an overdone lamb ("vulgar"), a refrigerated Camembert ("barbaric"), canned mushrooms ("contemptible"), and all those other culinary slipups and shortcuts toward which the classy palate shows no mercy. I have, on occasion, seen my husband stare into his glass of inconceivably unchilled white wine as if it were a direct personal assault on his integrity and his manhood.

Once in a great while, of course, we do run into a master chef, one of those superhuman hostesses who actually follow those Escoffier recipes which begin "bone 12 larks." This is the kind of lady who tirelessly scours the countryside in search of bran-fed chickens and butter freshly churned, and everything on her table—including the cloth —is made by hand.

On such an evening my husband trembles with pleasure and showers upon the architect of his joy the sort of admiring attention which, under any other circumstances, would have to be interpreted as a proposition. This happy experience, however, doesn't seem to blunt his critical edge—it is simply redirected against me.

As we walk to the car he will point out the perfection of the pâté, and wonder why I never trouble to make my own. Or he'll sigh mellowly over the moules marinières, noting, with unmistakable reproach in his voice, that "I hear she flew to Martha's Vineyard this morning so she could pick them fresh off the rocks."

Sometimes, in my fantasies, I am married to a meat-and-potatoes man, the type who only complains when he is given raspberry jello instead of lime. Our friends, no longer terrorized, deluge us with invitations, and the Escoffier ladies turn elsewhere for words of praise.

But reality takes over. He is frowning. The hollandaise is curdled, the asparagus canned. The hostess leans over to ask if something's the matter. And my husband the gourmet—thoroughly, explicitly, unsparingly—is about to tell her what all of those somethings are.

But my husband doesn't stop with telling hostesses. He tells busboys, waiters, chefs, and maître d's. And when the ice cream man rides down our street in summer, Milton will be happy to inform him that the quality of fudgicles has declined.

Now if he's doing all of this to other people, what do you think he's doing to his wife? Is he trying to crush my spirit? Is he persecuting me? No, he swears, he only wants to help.

Milton's notion of how to help me, however, is to drop a new recipe into my lap and say, "Here's an amusing way of preparing rabbit." But amusing to whom, I've never figured out, since these new recipes invariably involve no fewer than seven hours of cooking time and no fewer than 80 different ingredients, all of which must be purchased at no fewer than ten separate stores.

Another way that Milton tries to help me is by slipping into the kitchen when I'm not around, tasting whatever is cooking on the stove, and then—if you can imagine the nerve of the man—adding a little of this spice, a little of that.

"Who asked you?" I ask him. "How dare you!" I tell him. To which he will smugly reply, "I know that you will thank me in the end."

Furthermore, Milton insists on coming along with me to the butcher, where, with the shamelessness of a private eye, he probes and pokes and pinches, looking for plumpness in the chicken breasts, leanness in the beef, pinkness in the scallops of veal, and something he calls character in the pork roast.

"An artist," he explains, removing the frozen hamburger patties from my shopping cart and returning them to whence they came, "must work with first-class materials."

But I don't have any desire to be an artist, I tell him— and heaven knows I do not want his help. All I ask is to produce a meal that he and I will enjoy (not die with ecstasy over—just enjoy) and that the children will be willing (not *cheerfully* willing—sullenly willing will do) to consume.

Surely this is a great enough achievement in a family where it is more likely that Russia, China, and the United States will agree on eternal world peace than that Tony, Nick, and Alexander will agree on what they'd like to have for dinner.

But try explaining all of that to Milton, who feels that I'm shirking my culinary duties when I fail to serve the boys braised artichokes. Believe me, they don't want braised artichokes—they want SpaghettiO with 18 little meatballs. Or, as Nick warned me the last time I gave him a glorious gourmet experience, "You can make me put this bouillabaisse in my belly, but you can't make it stay there."

(And then there was the time I cooked that amusing rabbit dish and the children wanted to know what their dinner was. When they heard my answer, however, they dropped their forks and screamed in appalled unison, "A bunny! We're eating a little bunny!")

Perhaps I should be pleased that Milton wants to share the pleasures that he finds in fine cuisine.

But the kids are crying, my crêpe is stuck to the pan, and only Ronald McDonald can help me now.

In the course of his gourmet career, Milton has not merely alienated all of our friends, and every maître d', and the ice cream man, his children, and his wife. He has, in addition, alienated his wife's waistline, which—reeling from white sauces and brown sauces, from crème Anglaise and crème Chantilly—is not the waist it formerly used to be.

And so, from time to time, I start a diet, another diet, the diet-to-end-all-diets, the diet that will at last and forevermore strip the flesh from my bones and reduce me to a shriveled fragment of my current self.

I want it clearly understood, before I say another word, that I am not what anyone would ever call fat. But like several of the dieting ladies of my acquaintance—and I'm acquainted with plenty of them—I have a fantasy of physical perfection that is inextricably linked to the loss of a specific number of pounds.

In my case the magic number is eight, a mere eight pounds, which I presently hold responsible for the unfortunate condition of my waist, and for other inadequacies like inner-thigh fat, brassiere-strap bulge, and a rather nasty roll that plops into view above my snakeskin belt every time I buckle it on the third hole. The loss of eight pounds, I am convinced, would remedy all this, and furthermore, by some mystical process of redistribution, would cause two inches to drop from my hips onto the calves of my presently calfless legs. With such a vision of beauty hovering before me, it's small wonder that I have been, for years and years, a perennial dieter.

I don't want to be a perennial dieter, you understand. I

want to be a *former dieter*, now maintaining, with no effort at all, a dainty 117. Instead, I am perpetually starting diets, and often sticking to them, and on rare occasions actually achieving my diet goals. But never, having lost what I wanted to lose, am I capable of keeping it lost.

A couple of my friends are always asking me why I don't stop this diet nonsense and either get rid of the weight for good or learn to like it. But only a skinny friend could ask that question. As I look around at my sister sufferers, I have come to the gloomy conclusion that we are, one and all, perennial dieters and that for us dieting is not a short-term exercise in self-abnegation but a way of life.

It seems to go in six successive stages.

Stage 1: The Decision

You've been walking around for several weeks now eating everything in sight. In your innermost heart you know that there is far more to you than should be meeting the eye, but you lie to yourself, you make excuses, you run from your guilt.

And then one day you run smack into your great-aunt Jennie—she still thinks that anyone weighing less than 200 pounds is in the final phases of T.B.—and she says she can't get over how healthy you look.

Or you develop a great yearning to qualify for presently unwearable things like bikinis and hip-huggers, and things with bare (firm) midriffs and slits to the (unflabby) thigh, and things like the purple jersey dress you purchased when you were a far, far flatter person and into which you must pour yourself three weeks from Saturday night.

Or your son wants to know why the lady down the street is on a diet and you aren't.

Or your husband, who is a subtler fellow than your son, though not by much, keeps telling you about the magnificent body of the lady down the street.

Or maybe he just leans over, affectionately grabs a handful of some readily available segment of your flesh, and mutters, "Hmmm."

I know one woman who decided to diet after weeks of being troubled by a strange thwack-thwack-thwacking sound that seemed to follow her everywhere she went. "I finally discovered what it was," she said morosely. "The fat on my upper legs rubbing together."

Another friend of mine gave up food shortly after a depressing encounter with a full-length mirror. "I usually get ready for a mirror," she told me, "by tucking a little in here, a little in there. I lift my chin and stand up straight and, if I look very fast, I look pretty good." On that unfortunate occasion, however, she said, she came face to face with her image unprepared. "I was letting it all hang out," she explained with a shudder, "and was it hanging!"

The reasons for deciding that it's diet time are infinite. You go out shopping and discover that you're a size you've never been before. You get weighed and discover that you're a weight you've never seen before. Someone observes that you're growing more like your mother every day, and while you adore your mother she is, after all, Lane Bryant's best customer.

You may tell yourself that those corduroy pants were sized wrong and that spring scales are not to be trusted and that you definitely take after your father's side of the family. You may tell yourself anything you want—but suddenly you don't believe a word you're saying.

"This is it!" cries a voice deep inside you. "This is it!"

Stage 2: The Hiatus

Chances are that while your inner voice is crying this is it, your right hand is reaching for a second helping of blueberry pie. Strange as this may seem to the skinny outsider, it is no contradiction in terms. I've never met anyone who ever started a diet at the very moment she decided that she *would* start one. Diets are begun on Mondays, on New Year's Day, on birthdays, on the first day of the month, and in the morning. They are rarely begun between Christmas and New Year's Eve, in the middle of the week, or on a Sunday afternoon.

It is in the hiatus between decision and execution that the perennial dieter is truly at her happiest. Lying ahead is the path of perfect virtue, but in the blissful present there is only a guilt-free orgy of farewell-forever dining. "It's the last hot fudge sundae of my life," you say, with a sigh of supreme satisfaction. "It's the last double order of French fries I'll ever eat."

Stage 3: The Perfect Diet

Well before the advent of D day the perennial dieter has selected the perfect diet, a diet that is filling, painless, stomach-shrinking, good-habits-forming, and fast. Also nutritious enough, you hope, so you won't develop pellagra or pass out.

If, like me, you've been a dieter for the past ten years or more, you've already tried a dozen perfect diets. Certainly you must have had your fling with the egg-and-grapefruit diet, the high-protein diet, the low-protein diet, the high-fat-low-carbohydrate diet, the nothing-but-Metrecal diet, and the just-plain-nothing diet. You have followed regimens recommended by your family doctor, your favorite women's magazine, your diet club, your skinny neighbor, and the friend of a friend of a friend who lost 20 pounds in ten days on raw pickerel and mint leaves and she wasn't even hungry.

In the course of pursuing the perfect diet you have been compelled to develop a taste not only for raw pickerel but also for other tempting morsels such as broiled shredded-wheat biscuit and broccoli soup. You have learned how to count calories (half a cup of okra equals 30, a tablespoon of lime juice equals four), and you can weigh and measure a piece of lean meat down to the last seven-ninths of an ounce. You have, in addition, investigated jogging and sit-ups and Ping-Pong and sauna belts and a variety of electric devices in an effort to keep your muscles supple and firm as the flesh melts swiftly and permanently away, courtesy of the latest perfect diet.

Although your flesh has never melted swiftly and permanently away, you have managed somehow to cling to the conviction that somewhere the perfect diet is waiting for you. And, of course, you've found it again. It is the one on which a cousin went from size 12 to size six in less than 24 hours. It is the one where you drink a gallon of water five times a day. It is the one that shrinks your stomach so completely that just looking at a radish fills you up. Wiping the last of the cream puff from your lips, you face the future confident and unafraid.

Stage 4: Keeping the Faith

Okay, it's Monday and the first thing you do is place the bathroom scale two inches from the wall and one inch to the right of the towel rack because that's where it registers most accurately. Three inches to the left of the towel rack and flat against the wall, you're always a couple of pounds lighter—particularly if you lean back on your heels just a little—but you're finished with all that self-deception now. You are still allowed, however, to weigh yourself in the morning on an empty stomach, having removed your nightgown and stray bobby pins and, if you insist, your wedding ring. The daily weigh-in, some perennial dieters have discovered, may encourage them to stay on their perfect diet.

You may also be encouraged by such inspirational slogans as "Men never make passes at girls with fat bottoms" or "If a spineless meatball like Rita Schwartz can do it, so can I."

Telling your family and friends that you've started a diet may force you to stay on it, particularly if you've got the kind of family and friends who are likely to jeer and sneer at the first hint of defection. Fear of public humiliation has kept many a dieter dieting, though it also has driven many a dieter straight into the bathroom, where, with a running shower to cover the sound of chewing jaws, she can safely demolish a box of Mallomars.

Some dieters bolster their will with appetite-killing (and, occasionally, people-killing) pills, and I know one lady who actually sought the services of a hypnotist to control her unnatural passion for chocolates.

This hypnotist, she told me, led her to a vibrating couch, put her into what was presumably a trance, and announced that her favorite candies were prepared by nasty dwarfs who capered around a filthy cauldron tossing in vermin and other unpalatable ingredients. She was then sent off to the drugstore to buy as much candy as she desired—"You'll never be able to swallow it," the hypnotist said—and was halfway through a two-pound Whitman Sampler before realizing that she wasn't on her diet anymore.

As you've doubtlessly doped out for yourself by now, the best device for keeping the faith is to keep your distance from temptation. If, for example, you're on a two-week diet and you really mean business, you will refuse all dinner invitations during that period unless the hostess permits you to bring your own lamb chops. You will avoid restaurants too, because there is always the danger that while you're waiting for the dandelion greens with the low-calorie dressing you'll finish every roll in the breadbasket.

At home, of course, you have thoroughly stocked the kitchen with the requisite diet foods and, if husband and children will permit, have banished potato chips and Oreos from the house. You can't however, banish your husband from the house, and so you may have to endure the painful ordeal of cooking and watching him eat his gourmet meals while all you get to eat is a three-minute egg.

I have sometimes resolved this particular diet dilemma by persuading my husband that he needs a diet too—"Maybe your clothes don't feel tighter," I'll lie in my teeth, "but I think it's beginning to show around the jowls." As for feeding the kids, I simply avert my eyes when fixing the peanut butter sandwiches and pray for strength when I hand out the Popsicles.

If you've managed to stay on your diet for several days, you should now be starting to reap your first rewards. Already you can almost feel your long-lost hipbones, and faint hollows seem to be denting your apple cheeks. Suffused in a glow of pride and self-righteousness, you pat your diminished, albeit rumbling, stomach. "Eating," you say to all who care to listen, "is not the most important thing in life."

Stage 5: Defeat

So if eating is not the most important thing in life, why are you eating again? Why, after all those promises and privations, have you once more become a diet dropout? Are you morally as well as physically flabby? Are you weak of will, irresolute of purpose? Are you so undisciplined, so infantile, so *greedy*, that you can always be counted upon, sooner or later, to cave in at the sight of a Hershey bar with almonds, a freshly baked loaf of rye bread, a creamy, winy, buttery coquille Saint-Jacques?

The answer, of course, isn't nearly that simple. There are many different kinds of diet dropouts, each with her own *raison d'eat*. I have divided them into four categories: the alcoholic, the psychologist, the biologist, and the out-and-out quitter.

The alcoholic eater, like her drinking counterpart, is doomed from the moment she first slips off the wagon. Let her munch a single salted peanut and she's got to go on to devour the entire can. Let her nibble the tiniest forkful of strawberry cream tart, and within minutes all that's left is a faint pink smudge. In the life of the alcoholic eater there is no such thing as a taste or a sip, a spoonful or a slice. As soon as she succumbs to the seduction of "just one bite," she's had it.

When the psychologist goes off her diet, it's really her mother who's making her do all the eating. Her conversation is full of references to early-childhood traumas and the inexorable forces of the unconscious. "I'm having an anxiety attack," she says from behind her butterscotch sundae. "I'm feeling rejected. I'm searching for love."

The biologist who returns to full-time eating talks knowingly about sodium intake and metabolic rates and insists that she is not failing her diet but vice versa. "No matter how little I eat," she observes as she ladles the gravy onto her mashed potatoes, "everything I put in my mouth turns to fat."

The out-and-out quitter quits her diet because she can no longer endure reaching for a green-pepper ring when what she really wants to reach for is a mousse. She awakens in the night racked with hunger pains that no amount of celery stalks can assuage. She is sick of unpersuasive food substitutes such as mock potato pudding made with cauliflower, mock sour-cream sauce made with cottage cheese, mock malteds made with neither malt nor ice cream, and mock bloody Marys made with neither vodka nor gin. The will that has sustained her through lunch after lunch of beef bouillon with cucumber garnish slowly leaks away, and a life without éclairs no longer seems worth living.

As a frequent quitter, an occasional psychologist and biologist, and, now and then, an alcoholic, I would like to mention that there are times when the entire universe seems to conspire against the dieter. Holidays are part of the conspiracy, and so are vacations, anniversaries, and the hostess who serves me a pound of butter wrapped in a pastry crust and threatens to slash her wrists if I don't devour it. My husband is a conspirator when he talks me out of Greek salad and into moussaka. My best friend is a conspirator when she tells me that I already look too thin.

Assailed by such allurements and persuasions, even a stalwart dieter may defect. Saddest of all defectors is the lady who has stayed faithful for the entire 14 days or 21 days or three months necessary to lose the loathsome pounds. She has purchased a wardrobe commensurate with her two-sizes-smaller shape and she has just begun to think of herself as petite when—alas, alack, God damn!—she's pudgy again.

Stage 6: After the Fall

Here you are, you've broken your diet, and you'd better think of something to tell yourself fast. Don't worry. There are plenty of ways to deal with your failure and shame.

You can begin by persuading yourself that a person with such long lashes and such a nice nose doesn't need a slender body too. You can remind yourself that in an earlier, more perceptive era the Rubens nude was the ideal female form. You can then go on to contemplate your wit, your charm, and how smart your teachers said you were in college. You can look into your soul and decide you're a sensual woman, the kind who gives herself totally to all the grand passions like sex and food. Or you can look into your soul and decide you're a spiritual woman, too concerned with higher values to worry about weight.

When this self-appreciation starts wearing (you should pardon the expression) thin, you can divert yourself by projecting your secret self-hatred onto everyone else in sight. You can begin to hate skinny people who eat like football players and never gain an ounce. You can also hate skinny people who don't ever eat anything because, they complain, they just can't work up an appetite. You can hate fat people who think they're skinny and wouldn't dream of going on a diet. You can hate fat people who are still on the diet you just gave up.

If I were choosing someone to hate, it would be my friend Betsy, whose weight fluctuates wildly between 97 and 98 and who is probably a small size four. Betsy, like me, is a perennial dieter, though she never loses when she starves and never gains when she eats. She is, however, in a constant state of terror that obesity is just around the corner and swears that she'll go into seclusion if her scale ever hits the 100 mark. A finer human being might be able to sympathize with Betsy's fears, which, however bizarre, are quite sincere. But I'm not a finer human being, and I haven't weighed 97 since sixth grade, and you can't imagine how unsympathetic I am.

Eventually, inevitably, the diet dropout stops feeling hostile toward the rest of the world and starts feeling hostile toward herself. Suddenly you have a ghastly vision of turning into a 500-pounder in an extra-large muumuu rocking on the porch all alone because no one in the world could possibly love you. You gaze at your face in the mirror, and to your horror your nose appears to be broader, your lashes shorter. The body that in a more euphoric state you described as voluptuously Rubenesque you now describe in less permissive words. As for those comforting thoughts about your wit and intelligence and sensuality, they collapse under the assault of your self-criticism. You can't even hate a Betsy anymore.

It is only a matter of time now before some catalytic event will inspire you to try another diet. It will be, as it always is, the perfect diet. The ultimate diet. The diet-to-end-all-diets.

I'm starting mine on Monday. How about you?

XII

I Wasn't Meant to Be
One of the Groovy People

❦

I might become skinny, I might stop fighting with Milton, I might even stick to my New Year's resolutions. But no matter how I change my shape and try to mend my ways, I'll always be a middle-class girl from New Jersey.

Now as long as I'm home in the bosom of my family, I'm quite contented to be just who I am. But whenever I go on a visit to New York City, I suddenly yearn to be one of the Groovy People.

The trouble with defining a Groovy Person is that, as I sit myself down to write these very words, all that I've thought to be groovy is now ye-ecch. And when someone like me owns a Superman shirt and a Rocket Commander belt and something cute like a poster of Mao in the hallway, you'd better believe that their days in the groove are done.

(Note: Groovy People would never say "in the groove.")

Still, let me try to explain what makes a Groovy Person seem so appealing.

First of all, they always know what's happening. In fact, they know what's happening well before it has happened.

About four years ago, for instance, my New York girl friend Erica took me to an obscure boutique on the Lower West Side, where she bought three feathered belts and a feathered headband. Then she took me to an obscure boutique on the Lower East Side, where she bought 15 beaded necklaces and a peace pipe. Then she took me to an obscure back room on Broadway, where several squaws were working on buckskin dresses.

"Get some," she urged me everywhere we went. "Indians are going to be very big this season."

I explained to Erica that I'd thought the cowboys had won, and besides, I was too old to become an Indian. Needless to say, by the time feathers, beads, and buckskin were sweeping the country, and even my Aunt Florence was dressed like Pocahontas, my friend Erica had declared the fashion passé and was donating all of her purchases to the Cherokee.

The second distinctive quality about Groovy People is scorn—a pitiless, absolute scorn for all the Ungroovy.

(Note: Groovy People would never say "ungroovy.")

Let me tell you, there is a way my friend Sally has of remarking, "She's the type who still likes Simon and Garfunkel," that makes me want to go home and smash "Mrs. Robinson." She also has a way of saying, "Let's go to this groovy Mexican joint and eat enchiladas, unless you're still hung up on Fine French Food," that makes me want to go home and burn Julia Child.

Sally also knows that while it's okay to have a hammock in the dining room and an organ in the living room and a jukebox in the middle room and a set of whips in the bedroom, it is not okay to have a rotisserie in the kitchen. Don't ask me how she knows these things, but she does.

I suppose it's the same instinct that enables my friend Margo to perceive just exactly how old a Cadillac must become before it stops being vulgar and starts being charming.

The third thing about Groovy People is that they manage to avoid all of life's drab activities and to always do all of life's swinging things.

(Note: Groovy People no longer use the word "swinging.")

What I mean is, you never run into Groovy People in rented shoes and pedal pushers, surrounded by the hubby and some kids, working on a spare at Bowl America. Nor are Groovy People and family to be found shopping at the Safeway, attending the *Rumpelstiltskin* matinee, rowing a rowboat on the river, or watching how the planes take off at the airport.

Never, never.

Instead, Groovy People appear at opening nights, and at parties raising funds for groovy causes, and at chic little boîtes that are so chic and little that sometimes the owner won't even let them in. They also march in all the major demonstrations, though they don't, as their detractors like to claim, carry a banner which reads "Groovy People Against the Vietnam War."

As for their children, Groovy People do not associate with them until they're old enough to be Groovy Kids. In fact, they won't even associate with their husband, unless he's the type whose hair stylist comes to his office.

I've felt grateful, all these years, to be so patiently tolerated by the Groovy People I know in New York City.

They tell me how to dress and what to subscribe to, and where I should go for the weekend and who I should go with.

They've managed to make me terribly discontented.

What they haven't done, alas, is make me groovy.

While I may have a wistful wish or two to be as groovy as Erica or Sally, I don't really want to develop a whole new life-style. If folks want to live on communes, eat organic foods, join the revolution, or picket for Women's Lib, I'd never object—I'm willing to say "Right on!" But if I happen to prefer a more middle-class existence, why must they sneer?

For it's perfectly lovely the way everyone is doing his own thing, but how come they think their own thing's so much better than mine?

If I'd rather collect for Heart Disease than raise unsprayed tomatoes, does this have to be taken as proof that I'm . . . unworthy?

It seems that it does.

At a recent cocktail party, for instance, I met this mustachioed fellow—dressed in fringe and a beatific smile—who was sounding off on the glories of rural simplicity. (I've noticed lately that a lot of folks who only a year ago were declaring that it was our moral obligation to dwell in the heart of the urban crisis are now touting the virtues of a pig farm with outdoor plumbing.)

Anyway, he was planning, he announced, to leave for Vermont in the morning with a band of his fellow communards.

"I want real relationships with real people in a real place," he explained.

"That's beautiful," I said.

"I want to stop expanding my income and start expanding my consciousness," he told me.

"That's beautiful," I said.

"I want to dine on bread I baked myself, and read by candles I made myself, and dress in simple garments I sewed with my own two hands."

"That's beautiful," I said. "Tell me, did you yourself sew that fringed vest you are wearing?"

"Well," he answered, "not exactly. But I bought it at the Ethnic Ecology Boutique for only $79.95, of which two percent will go to the save-the-purple-grackle fund."

"That's beautiful," I said.

As you can see, I was being terribly understanding about his doing his own thing. But I could tell he disapproved of me doing mine.

"I suppose," he told me, "that a life of wall-to-wall carpets and meaningless human contacts is all you were taught to want.

"And I suppose," he continued, "that you were never given the opportunity to develop the grandeur of spirit, the refined sensibilities, the magnificence of soul that living in a commune requires.

"And I suppose," he said, his lip curling ever so slightly, "that some people just don't have it."

I glanced around the room, pretending to search for those people who just didn't have it. But I knew damn well that the people he meant was me.

I encountered a similar put-down at a recent demonstration, when one intense young marcher turned to me and declared, "I gave up haircuts in February to protest our involvement in Vietnam."

"Fantastic," I said.

We sang a few peace songs and then he confided, "I gave up shoes in March to protest racism at home and abroad."

"Fantastic," I said.

We handed out a few leaflets and then he added, "I gave up food last week to protest air pollution, water pollution, noise pollution, and the population explosion."

I told him that was fantastic too, convinced that we had established this swell rapport. But then the demonstration broke up and I happened to mention that I was taking my kids for haircuts and sneakers, after which we were going to stop for cheeseburgers.

My new friend drew away from me, repelled. "Hawk!" he shrieked. "Fascist! *Housewife!*"

That last crack really stung. Why was he picking on me? Why wasn't being a housewife doing *my* thing?

I found out why when a Women's Lib group asked me to picket a men's clothing store on the grounds that it only sold men's clothing. I replied that while I admired their persistence and imagination, I couldn't break my appointment with my gynecologist.

"Let your husband go to the gynecologist," they urged. "Doesn't he *ever* help around the house?"

I told them that he helped lots—with the dishes and the cleaning and with getting all the kids off to school in the morning—and that I really couldn't complain.

"You just don't realize how miserable and rotten your existence is," they answered. "If you don't start complaining and objecting and protesting and striking back, you'll never get to do your own thing."

Oh yes I will.

I am, in fact, doing it right this minute—if they'd only leave me alone and let me enjoy it.

But, of course, they *won't* leave me alone.

The commune types can't understand that I can scarcely

bear sharing a bathroom with my family, much less with a houseful of communards in Vermont.

And the demonstrators can't understand that it might indeed be possible for me to oppose war, racism, pollution, and overpopulation—and still eat lunch.

And the Women's Liberation women can't understand that I might already be (my own kind of) liberated.

And now my friend Dorothy can't understand that I don't even want to achieve self-actualization. (Actually, I never knew I didn't want to achieve it, until she started explaining what it was.)

Dorothy, you see, has just returned from California where, for only $700 plus plane fare, she was able to spend two whole weeks sobbing, screaming, hugging, punching, crawling around on her knees crying "Mama," dancing in the moonlight shouting "Oogla," and exposing her most intimate emotions to a bunch of perfect strangers doing likewise.

"Is that what Disneyland is really like?" I asked her.

Dorothy sighed. "Now don't pretend," she told me, "that you haven't heard of Encounter Groups. They're sweeping the country. They're going to save us all."

"Save us from what?" I said.

Dorothy reached out her hand and touched my cheek gently. "Poor Judy," she said. "You're blind, you're deaf, you're numb, you're practically dead—and you don't even know it."

"Is there anything else I don't know?" I asked, rather tartly.

Yes, there was. "And you're full of guilt and shame and fear and hate."

"Are you finished yet?" I asked, a little more tartly.

No, she wasn't. "And you feel desperately unlovable and unloved."

(*125*)

"But outside of that I'm in marvelous shape—right?" I said, hoping to discourage further discussion.

Dorothy, unfortunately, has never discouraged easily. "Don't worry," she said, throwing her arms around me and holding me tight. "There's still hope."

I tried to pry her fingers off my shoulders. "Cut it out, Dorothy," I said. "You're hurting me."

"Of course I'm hurting you," she replied triumphantly. "Love hurts. Feelings cause pain. But when you're ready to give and accept those painful feelings, you'll find Joy."

"That's what you learned in your Encounter Group?" I asked. "For only $700 plus plane fare?"

"Don't be so cerebral," Dorothy said. "Stop thinking. Start experiencing. Communicate with emotions instead of with words."

I communicated by making a face at her, and the next thing I knew Dorothy had picked up some throw pillows and was throwing them at me.

"What was that all about?" I yelled, as I dodged the last pillow.

Dorothy smiled. "I was feeling a little hostile toward you just now," she said, "and I needed to express it. Anything verbal would have been dishonest."

I congratulated her on her honesty and carefully kept my distance. "Tell me," I said, "did you throw a lot of things in California?"

"I certainly did," Dorothy said with pride. "And I gave one woman a terrific black eye because she reminded me of my second grade teacher."

"That really is terrific," I said. "I suppose your group was very pleased with you."

Dorothy blushed modestly. "As a matter of fact," she said, "there was a spontaneous outburst of applause."

I was getting uneasy. "So what else did you do in your

Encounter Group?" I asked. "Besides assaulting helpless people, I mean."

"Well," said Dorothy. "I chanted. I fantasized. I regressed. I stripped myself bare psychologically. And, oh yes, I spent a day and a half contemplating an apple core. It was an unforgettable experience."

This unforgettable experience, I calculated, probably cost about 75 bucks, but I didn't think I ought to bring that up. "I can't wait to hear about it," I said instead, not wanting to inspire more hostility.

Dorothy was happy to oblige. "I discovered," she said, her voice aquiver with reverence, "that the core of every apple has its own individuality, and that no two apple cores are alike."

I nodded knowingly and Dorothy went on.

"And once you recognize the uniqueness of every apple core," she said, "you come to recognize the uniqueness of each and every human being."

"Ain't that the truth," I murmured.

Dorothy glared at me. "If you're going to be like that," she scolded, "you will never achieve spiritual growth and self-actualization. You will never enlarge your sensory awareness. You will never find Joy."

I shrugged my shoulders. "For $700 plus plane fare," I said, "maybe I'll just settle for Acapulco."

XIII

Two Weeks in Another Town

❧❦❧

I don't get many trips to Acapulco. I've never—come to think of it—had *one*. But I can't complain for, over the years, I've had my share of vacations.

Maybe, come to think of it, *more* than my share.

And it's time once again for another summer vacation—just me and Milton, the kids, a mother's helper, and 25 house guests.

It's time once again to refresh ourselves at the shore, with sparkling sands, a pounding surf, red sails in the sunset, and an overflowing septic tank in the yard.

It's time once again for two weeks in another town, for fun-filled days in another rented beach house, for the kind of togetherness that teaches a family the joys of being apart.

I'm afraid I know exactly what I'm getting into.

Milton rises early on Saturday morning to pick up the U-Haul—a five-foot-long orange monstrosity that is, in effect, a small truck. I keep telling myself we wouldn't need the U-Haul if we owned a sensible family-sized station wagon instead of a cramped and moth-eaten '65 Ford. But that probably isn't true. I doubt whether anyone has yet designed an automobile large enough to accommodate all the things we can't live without for 14 days.

Like, three bicycles, two typewriters, one television set, my copper pots (I don't understand other people's pots), my steam iron (I don't understand other people's irons), a phonograph, and a few dozen records.

As well as, five cartons of medical supplies, five cartons of books and toys, three boys' worth of balls, bats, rafts, mats, and roller skates, and the mother's helper's tennis racket and surfboard.

In addition to, one Dynel braid, one Dynel chignon, one Dynel wig, assorted rollers, one hair drier, one hair blower, and, if all else fails, one very big hat.

Not to mention, everyone's clothes, 90 towels, lots of sheets and pillowcases, lots of sleeping bags, and—oh, yes—my son the guitarist's guitar.

"It won't fit," Milton tells me, looking over the pileup out on the sidewalk. "Something's got to give. Let's forget about the phonograph, okay?"

"Why don't we just forget about me?" I reply, always cooperative. "Whoever heard of not taking a phonograph?"

Milton considers the problem once again. "I'll tell you what," he says. "You don't really need all that hair stuff. We won't be going out anywhere fancy, you know."

I give him one of my how-could-you-you-beast looks.

And then, "Are you trying to tell me," I ask him, "that on this vacation—which, I'd like to remind you, happens to be my vacation and not only yours—I'm supposed to be cooking three times a day for 14 days of unrelieved drudgery without once being taken out to a nice restaurant?"

Milton sighs. "We'll bring the hair stuff."

After jamming everything into the U-Haul (somehow we always do), the six of us jam ourselves into the car—two of the kids and the mother's helper in back, the two of us and the other kid in front. It should be noted that each boy gets to ride in the front seat for precisely one third of the journey, and heaven help us if our calculations are wrong.

We're off.

On our summer vacations there have been bad trips and worse trips, but nothing that would ever persuade me that getting there is half the fun.

Among my blacker memories is a two-day safari from Washington to Cape Cod, when we stopped to visit my family in New Jersey. Milton parked on the street, and then, when we were getting ready to leave, we discovered that (a) a light-blue Chevy had parked in front of us, and that (b) Milton didn't know how to back up the U-Haul. (I might mention that Milton had said we shouldn't stop to visit, and I had said he should put the car in a parking lot.) Anyway, several hours later, having finally located the owner of the light-blue Chevy by ringing every doorbell in Maplewood, we continued on our journey, in what must be inadequately described as an atmosphere of mutual reproach.

Last August's trip to the beach in Delaware, on the other hand, was far shorter, but—to compensate—rain leaked through the holes in our convertible top from portal to portal. Furthermore, the horn dropped into Milton's lap about five minutes after we'd set off, so I was in charge of sticking my head out the window and yelling "Beep!" whenever a beep was called for.

Over the years I've concluded that the best way to travel with kids is to keep them up as late as possible the night before so they'll sleep part of the way, and to feed and entertain them the rest of the time so they'll be too busy to slash each other up.

It is my habit to pack enough emergency rations so that if we should take a wrong left turn and wind up in the Sahara, we could still dine in luxury for a month. As for the entertainment, there is lots of coloring in coloring books and much singing from *The Fireside Book of Children's Songs*. There is also a terrific contest that Daddy invented, which goes, "The first boy to see a giraffe gets five cents."

But all this food and frolic, I'm afraid, doesn't stop the elbow in the ribs, the knee in the groin, the pokes and pinches, and shoves, which seem to be the inevitable consequence of putting three small boys into one small space for more than 30 seconds. Nor does it discourage them from the need to make a comparative study of every men's room between here and wherever we're going.

I have been quite successful, however, at discouraging car sickness. "No Viorst," I tell my boys, "has ever in his life gotten sick in a car." Unfortunately, this inspirational slogan doesn't work with the mother's helper, who is invariably unable to help mother because she is greenly leaning out of the back window taking deep, desperate gasps of fresh air.

Last year, though, she wasn't leaning out the back window. *He* was.

What happened is that I had become tired of sharing my summer vacations with sexy young girls and decided to switch to sexy young boys instead. I figured that 15-year-old Benjy would be the perfect mother's helper because he'd had plenty of practice with his own younger brothers and sisters and because, as a fellow fellow, he'd be able to teach our three boys all sorts of manly arts, like how to row boats and catch crabs.

Which he did. The trouble is, he also taught them a few other manly arts, like how to come out of a shower dirtier than when you went in and how to make yourself burp at will.

The 15-year-old girls I used to hire never taught wicked things like that. Still, there was something about their beautiful blooming bodies in those Kleenex-sized bikinis that I found strangely disturbing.

I explained to myself that I shouldn't be disturbed. But the day I watched Mary Elizabeth as she gazed worshipfully at my beloved husband and said, "For an older person you sure know how to groove," while beloved husband contracted his stomach muscles and smoothed down his hair where it thins, I decided that I was boycotting nymphets.

The best part about a male mother's helper, however, is not that he won't make passes at my husband, but that he can share a bedroom with my boys. This is quite important since, in the interests of economy, the houses we rent every summer tend to be small—if not downright dwarfed. (Another thing I've got against Mary Elizabeth is that the summer she worked for us, *she* slept in her own private chamber while Milton and I wound up on the living-room couch.)

Not only are our summer houses small; they're also inclined to be somewhat less than luxurious. I hate to sound like a spoiled American housewife, but I'm afraid I'm pitifully dependent on things like hot water, a toilet that actually flushes when you flush it, a mattress that is not stuffed with old socks, and an oven from which clouds of black smoke do not issue.

Since all of our rentals are made on the phone, sight unseen, we can always count on their possessing some interestingly unsavory features.

One year, for instance, our summer dream house was, in the words of the real-estate agent, "situated in the heart of a magnificent woodland brimming with natural wonders." What she forgot to mention, however, was that the outstanding natural wonder of our magnificent woodland was a tribe of mosquitoes the size of full-grown sparrows. During those two weeks, it probably cost our family a quart of blood to get through the woods to the beach.

Another year, the boys were quartered in an unfurnished cellar-playroom, where they were supposed to sleep in sleeping bags on the floor. It was a perfectly fine arrangement—except that the playroom suffered from something called "upward seepage," which meant that water rose from the ground to the floor and thence into the sleeping bags. On a bad seepage night we'd awake to discover that three damp and shivering boys had joined us in bed.

In our more affirmational moments, however, we always try to take the position that the house itself is quite beside the point. What really, really counts, of course, is the ocean —that's why we're there in the first place, is it not?—and as long as the weather holds up, so the theory goes, we can live a sea-tossed, sun-kissed life outdoors.

According to our Basic Summer Concept, the grown-ups sleep late while the kids and the mother's helper tiptoe down to the shore, where, around 11 A.M., we join them, to lounge on our deck chairs and read trashy novels all day, while the sun shines upon us and soft breezes blow and childish laughter is heard—far in the distance.

But I'm afraid this Basic Concept has basic flaws.

In the first place, by the time the children have tiptoed out of the house, knocking over several pieces of furniture and screaming at top volume, "Shut up, dumbhead, or you'll wake up Mom and Dad," Mom and Dad are irredeemably awake.

In the second place, at any given moment down at the beach, Anthony will be going under for the third time and Nick will be burying Alexander alive in the sand and the mother's helper will be engrossed in a deep conversation with several other teen-agers whose charges are also about to meet their Maker.

Which makes it rather hard to read.

It seems to me that when I'm not standing at the edge of the ocean crying, "Come back. Come back. You're going to drown! Come back before it's too late," I'm kissing jellyfish stings and rebuilding inundated castles. Or I may be asking my husband, in a spirit of genuine curiosity, "Why is it that I'm building castles and rescuing children from a watery grave while you're just lying around doing nothing?"

Please believe me, you don't want to hear his answer.

The third and most basic flaw in our Basic Concept is that the sun, on summer vacations, does not always shine.

No, it does not. One morning you wake up to the sinister sound of raindrops on the roof. You're very unhappy. The next morning you hear the same sound. You're very, very unhappy. And on the third morning (by which time you and the children have exhausted Monopoly, storybooks, bowling, kiddie movies, working with clay, and hide-and-seek), if you're still getting it from the great rainmaker in the sky, hysteria sets in.

All these deviations from our Basic Concept impose certain strains on our happy marriage, which, even under the best of summer circumstances, has trouble staying happy during vacation.

You see, there's Milton, with time on his hands and not much to do but notice that he doesn't admire the way I do things.

"Where the hell did you learn to make a bed?" he likes to

ask. He also likes to point out that there's sand in the sheets, as well as in his undershorts, the toothpaste, and the egg salad. But, as I like to point out right back, there is just so much sand that one human being can cope with, and if he can't stand it he can . . .

Well, you can imagine where this sort of discussion—and the one about "How come the beach towels are always soggy?" and the one about "Hot dogs for supper? Again? And on paper plates?"—could lead. Rediscovering each other on summer vacation isn't anywhere near as beautiful as you might think.

What saves us from each other is the arrival of all those people to whom we tossed out the most casual invitations before we left town. "We've got plenty of room. Come and see us," we're always saying to friends, neighbors, and strangers we meet at cocktail parties.

And they do. Lots of them. Simultaneously. With their babies, their portable cribs, their pregnant cats, their food fetishes, and their sun allergies. Hoping we won't mind if they make a couple of long-distance phone calls. Hoping we won't mind if they leave the baby with us for just a few hours while they dash over to visit So-and-So. Hoping we won't mind serving them breakfast in bed.

Actually, most of our house guests are perfectly lovely people. The real problem is that they do tend to arrive all at once. One lively weekend back in '69, we established some sort of hospitality record by putting up—in our tiny two-bedroom house—one family of four, one family of three, and one poor misguided cousin who, he told us, had accepted our kind invitation because he badly needed a little peace and quiet.

But peace and quiet are awfully hard to come by when you're spending your summer vacation with three busy boys. I can sit on the porch at twilight with a gin and tonic in my hand, listening to the roar of the surf and the strum of the crickets and thinking that I've finally found serenity —and you can bet your last nickel that some small weeping kid will soon be at my side saying, "Is paint remover poison?" or, "Something with a terrible smell is leaking," or, "We lost Alexander."

In all our years of going to the shore, I have never yet failed to require the services of the local doctor, the local plumber, and the local police. I guess I'm just not destined for serenity.

And yet, despite our vacation's imperfections, we're always sorry to see it come to an end. We're sorry because we do adore the beach, but we're also sorry because, for three full days before our departure, we have to put the house back together again.

I'm not talking now about dusting and sweeping and defrosting and scrubbing and such. That's easy enough. No, I'm talking about the stuff of which lawsuits are made, about repairs involving the screen door through which Nick, in a game of tag, happened to dive, and the mantelpiece which—when climbed upon in a game of follow-the-leader—proved unequal to the weight of three healthy boys. I'm talking about the painting over the couch that got in the way of a water-pistol fight. I'm talking about the teeth marks in the table (God knows why), the footprints on the ceiling (God knows how), and the missing maple chest in the children's bedroom (God knows where).

Everyone, even the mother's helper, is expected to help me resurrect the house. The other sacrifice everyone is asked to make is in the area of eating—all the food in the kitchen must be consumed.

Maybe you don't consider this such a sacrifice. But then, maybe nobody ever served you a casserole made of sour cream, mustard, and bean dip.

Every year, on the final night of vacation, it's been our

custom to hold a small family ceremony. Milton buys a bottle of champagne, and even Alexander gets to drink some. The boys love the part when the cork pops off with a bang, but they love even more the opportunity to propose a farewell toast.

"I want to drink," said Anthony last summer, "to finally having my own bed with no pesty brothers in it." (Cries of indignation and the clinking of glasses.)

"And I want to drink," said Nick, "to holding my breath under water for ten minutes." (Cries of "Big liar" and the clinking of glasses.)

"And I want to drink," said Alexander, "to the bunny I saw in the yard, and the fish I saw in the ocean, and the sand castle that was still there the next day."

I remember leaning over and giving my tipsy young son a great big hug.

And I remember promising myself to never forget that this was what summer vacations were all about.

Now it's all very nice, over pink champagne, to turn misty-eyed on the subject of family vacations. But there are times when Milton and I, desperate to flee the coloring books and the Flintstones, must go on a vacation of our own.

I understand that a trip for two is supposed to give a terrific lift to your marriage, even if you're married to each other. It somehow never works that way with us.

You see, traveling isn't one of those things we do well together. Lovebirds though we may be the whole year long, as soon as we pack our suitcase, hostility begins to fill our hearts.

To be more exact, hostility begins to fill our hearts *while* we're packing our suitcase, because Milton has a tendency to tuck his muddy shoes, and the after-shave lotion that leaks, between my two best dresses. He also has the audacity to tell me I don't *need* my two best dresses, or the 11 others I've packed, or the bathing suit I'm taking in case there's a 70° rise in the temperature, or the ball gown I'm taking in case we're asked to a ball.

There's an obvious solution to this little problem—separate suitcases—but just try explaining that to a man who, contemplating the costs of overweight baggage, has adopted the nasty motto "Travel light." Mine, as you may have guessed, is "Never leave behind that which you might need, no matter how unlikely it is that you'll need it."

The product of this conflict in philosophies is a large amount of clothes in a very small space—and his leaky lotion.

By the time we've snapped the lock on our mangled belongings, we are already asking ourselves why we ever got married in the first place. It won't be the last time we're moved to raise this question.

I needn't mention the horrors of the plane trip itself, except to say that I always take two sleeping pills, and he always falls asleep. There are occasions when it's a very lovely experience to gaze upon the slumbering face of the man you adore—but not when you're landing by radar.

"Wake up and stop this plane from crashing," I snarl in his ear. He tells me what he thinks of this request.

Things do not improve on the ground. They do not improve because Milton is very nonchalant about accommodations. "A hotel room," goes another of his mottos, "is nothing but a place to hang your hat."

I'll tell you what he means by that.

A few years ago we went to France on one of those bargain-rate, charter-flight, see-Europe-on-a-quarter-a-day deals. I'm not saying that our hotel in Paris was a flophouse exactly, but when Milton asked whether any rooms were available, the concierge replied, "Not just now, Monsieur. But come back in about 20 minutes and there will be."

And so there was—five do-it-yourself flights up—with no heat, no hot water, a flourishing insect life, and a bathroom down the hall which we shared with 50 million Frenchmen. It was Milton's cheerful position that the Eiffel Tower was worth a few bedbugs, and that if I died of pneumonia in that freezing fifth-floor room, I'd die smiling, for at least I'd seen the Louvre.

That was not my position at all.

"You aren't a very spiritual person, are you?" he said, when I'd told him my position on his position.

"How," I sobbed, "can a person be spiritual without her own bathroom?"

Once we'd gotten over the packing hurdle and the flying hurdle and the hotel hurdle, you'd think we'd have nothing to do but enjoy ourselves, right? Wrong!

How should we enjoy ourselves? *Who's* going to decide how we should enjoy ourselves? What makes *him* think that he can tell *me* how *I* should enjoy myself?

You get the idea.

He wants to go to the Bibliothèque Nationale and contemplate the Napoleonic era. I want to go to Pierre Cardin and contemplate a coat.

He wants to walk in the rain down the Champs Élysées. I tell him I just had my hair done and couldn't possibly.

He has this insane idea that we should rent bicycles and spend a week biking through the wine country. I tell him I'm leaving on the next plane.

It's with great relief we return to the kids and the dishes, the stopped-up drain and the out-of-order phone. In a month or so, we're even speaking again.

We're even, as the bitter memories dim, able to draw this positive conclusion: That any marriage can make it through flood and through fire, through illness, recession, the presence of mothers-in-law. But now that ours has survived the joys of travel, we're certain that it can survive just about anything.

It has sometimes been suggested that Milton and I may be temperamentally unfit to take vacations. Surely, say our friends, we'd be happier, more healthy human beings if we simply gave them up and stayed at home.

But why should we? All over America—indeed, all over the world—people are returning from woods and mountains, from foreign lands and Caribbean isles, refreshed both in body and in soul. Someday, somehow—or so we still believe—we will too.

A while ago, in fact, we planned what we'd hoped would be the perfect vacation—five carefree days in Puerto Rico. We'd fly to San Juan (he said that I could even bring my own suitcase), we'd check into a charming hotel (he said that I could even have my own bathroom), and we'd turn our backs on the world—basking by day in the tropical glow of the sun and basking by night in the tropical glow of a pineapple-coconut-rum drink called piña colada.

We would get away from it all.

And so we did, all the way from Dulles Airport to the hotel. Ah, but there, waiting at the desk when we arrived, was an urgent message from our ever-efficient baby-sitter, Sheila Clarke.

EMERGENCY, it said. CALL AT ONCE.

"I hope you folks aren't planning to spend any money down there," said Sheila cheerfully, when we got her on the line. "The bank just phoned that you're $200 overdrawn."

Milton, I must concede, didn't bat an eyelash. "Tell them," he said, "that they've made a terrible mistake."

"Is that possible?" Sheila asked.

"I doubt it," Milton replied, "but it ought to keep them busy till we get back."

We then went down to the cocktail lounge, where I ordered a piña colada to calm my nerves. Halfway through my third piña colada, I had become persuaded that the bank owed *us* $200.

The next day I was on the beach early to take advantage of the sunshine, covered only by Sea & Ski and the blue bikini I had decided to purchase despite the saleslady's cruel and crushing remarks.

("You're not big," she'd coolly observed when I'd tried on the suit. "But you sure are soft.")

Well . . . there I lay, spread-eagled on the sand, when a bellhop suddenly appeared at my side, breathing heavily. I thought my bikini was affecting his nervous system, but no such luck. He was, alas, out of breath from running over to bring me more ill tidings.

"A Miss Clarke is on the phone," he told me. "She says it's an emergency."

And there was our Sheila again, eager to notify me that our Ford needed a new transmission and that our washing machine needed a new motor and that torrential rains back home had flooded our basement.

Fortunately, there was a bar right there on the shore, to which Milton gently led me. By the fourth piña colada he was explaining to me that washing machines and cars, left to their own devices, would heal themselves. By my fourth piña colada, I was even believing him.

The next afternoon, about 4:30, as I sat on our darling balcony smiling at palm trees, the telephone rang.

"I thought you would want to know . . ." Sheila began.

"No," I interrupted. "I would not want to know. Honestly I wouldn't. Do I have to?"

Sheila, who marches to her own drummer, pretended I hadn't said a word. ". . . that your portable TV was stolen while I was downstairs bailing out water from the basement."

"Are you finished now?" I asked, very unpleasantly. "May I hang up?"

"Also, someone was stabbed down at the end of the block, but no one we know."

I slammed down the receiver without saying good-bye and called room service. "Please send up five piña coladas," I said. "It's an emergency."

By Saturday, though my body was golden brown, I was very pale in my soul. I knew the phone would ring again—and it did.

"You told me to be sure to let you know as soon as Alexander got accepted at nursery school," said Sheila.

I swear I never told her any such thing, but I didn't mind hearing a little good news.

"That's nice," I said.

"You don't understand," said Sheila. "The school wrote that he was very intelligent for his age and that he had a very outgoing personality and that you should try again next year when he's more manageable."

Six piña coladas later, I decided that I hadn't failed as a mother after all.

It was Sunday and we were checking out of our hotel, when dear dear Sheila called for the final time. "Nick just had some stitches put in his finger where it was crushed in the door," she said, "but we'll try to pick you up at the airport anyhow."

I told her that would be lovely.

But I also told her I wasn't coming home, unless she showed up with a pitcher of piña coladas.

XIV

The Reason It's Worth It

❧⚬❧

In the end it probably isn't disaster that drives a housewife to drink, but the simple wear and tear of everyday life.

Married life. Wherein Nick can't find his library book or Anthony clean pants; and Milton hogs three-fourths of our double bed.

Married life. Wherein the most important decision that I had to make this week was whether to wax the floors on Thursday or Friday.

Married life. Wherein I've already been responsible for 19 Halloween costumes, 22 birthday parties, 85 fights with my husband (I'm blaming him for the other 3,015), and the dispensing of half a million chocolate-chip cookies.

Married life. Is it worth it? Yes, it's worth it. Yes, it is.

It's worth it because that man in my bed is the man I still want to be there. It's worth it because that man still makes me feel loved.

It's my birthday, and when I awake, Milton greets me with a tender kiss, a dozen roses, and a bottle of my favorite perfume. Gazing fondly into my sleep-swollen eyes, he swears that I'm even lovelier than I was on the day he married me. After bringing me my breakfast on a tray, he urges me to buy a new dress ("Expense is no object, my darling") to wear at the elegant restaurant he's taking me to that evening. And then, when evening comes, and we're sipping champagne and toying with the pâté, and the violins are playing—at his request—a medley of old movie themes, he leans forward and whispers huskily, "I love you."

Forget it. My husband doesn't behave that way and neither, I'll bet, does yours. Furthermore, if they did, chances are we'd conclude that they were either cracking up or overcompensating for something unspeakably extramarital.

For a husband has many, many ways of making a wife feel loved, but he almost never does it with champagne and roses. And even though I, now and then, may dream those birthday dreams, I will happily settle for love in its many oblique and unglamorous manifestations, for "I love you" can be translated into his willingness to lace my ski boots, and to listen to my discussion of infant diarrhea, and to say —at least in public—that my position on Foreign Aid makes perfect sense, and to not say anything at all when I've just done something spectacularly stupid.

One way he makes me feel loved is by making sacrifices for me—and I don't mean valiant rescues from burning buildings. Almost anyone will rescue a lady from a burning building, but only a loving husband puts down his newspaper, puts on his galoshes, and trudges into the sleet and the hail because his wife has smoked her last cigarette and doesn't expect to survive until morning.

And then there are those times when I'm in bed, and he's scrunched under the blankets almost asleep, and I can't sleep because I need some water, and he climbs out of bed and brings me water.

And those times when I spill the coffee grounds all over the kitchen floor, and he gets out the broom and sweeps them up.

Another way that Milton shows me I'm loved is by tolerating my small peculiarities. Now of course I expect him to live with the fact that I spray my spray on his comb, and hang his trousers on wire, not wooden, hangers. But I'm speaking of really *peculiar* peculiarities, which only a loving husband would endure.

For instance:

I like to arrive at railroad stations an hour before departure time, just in case there is a sudden, unannounced revision of the schedule and the train leaves early. It is Milton's contention that no train ever, in the history of the railroads, has left early; but I am not interested in historical approaches to travel. I tell him please, it's 1:45, and the train is due to go exactly at three, and it's a 15-minute drive to the station, so let's get out of here. And if he takes me when I ask him to take me (though *he* knows and *I* know that I am psychopathic on the subject), I feel utterly, inexpressibly cherished. And if he makes me wait until 2:35, and we arrive at the station only ten minutes before departure time, I feel rejected, misunderstood, and unloved.

One of my very good friends, for another for instance, has a thing about roaches, which is not like your thing and mine but a terror that goes beyond reason. She has been known to drag her husband off long-distance phone calls, out of showers, and—once—home from a business conference, to step on one of these pests. Her husband has patiently pointed out that if she stepped on the cockroach herself it absolutely would *not* sink its teeth into her foot, and that if she chose to ignore it, it would under no circumstances attack her; but deep down in her heart she doesn't believe him. And so he has become her slayer of roaches, an act of love that, as far as she's concerned, beats a dozen long-stemmed roses every day.

Well, maybe these aren't among your major hangups, but I'll bet you've got some interesting ones of your own. And whenever a husband chooses to indulge them, we feel that he, in effect, is saying to us, "This is asinine. This is absurd. This is impossible! But I'll put up with it because I happen to love you."

There are women who maintain that they can manage to feel loved without water in the middle of the night and without roach slayers. But can any of us manage without some kind of husbandly reassurance that we are, indeed, the kind of person we're trying so hard to be—whether it's stunningly gorgeous or stunningly smart, whether it's fabulous mother or fabulous cook, whether it's sex goddess of the Western World or the best grower of roses in the garden club . . . or one of each? It's here, in this tricky realm of reassurance, that most of our husbands tend to go astray.

I am still brooding about a certain Christmas Day when I was seven months pregnant, weighed enough to be nine months pregnant, and felt about as desirable as an upholstered chair. After the children had rampaged through their gifts, I sat down to open my husband's present to me, which was packaged in a handsome striped box with a big gold bow.

Murmuring something appropriately coy, I peeked inside, and there . . . there upon the lavender tissue paper was a long-sleeved high-necked extra-heavy yellow flannel nightgown that could only be described as "serviceable."

Serviceable! Well, that's what you are, you fat pregnant lady, you, I told myself, and promptly—to my husband's total bewilderment—burst into tears.

What did I want? I wanted a useless size-eight see-through nightie, which would say that I was utterly enticing—great big belly and all. For though it's nice to be told you're attractive when you weigh 125, it's vital when you weigh 157.

And the fact is that, despite that Christmas error, my husband grasps this notion very well. And when I'm in sweatsocks, and no makeup, and the apron covered with yesterday's dinner stains, and he comes behind me and gives me a kiss on the neck, he's saying, "You're sexy" and also saying, "You're loved."

Although I tend to be particularly sensitive about the state of my sexual attractiveness, it is by no means my only area of vulnerability. Too many times, as I rush from the supermarket to the pediatrician, I begin to get the feeling that my college-educated brains are slowly rotting away and that I will soon have nothing worth communicating to anyone over the age of ten. There are days I completely lose track of the latest coup, and the latest war, and the current situation in Southern Rhodesia. Then loving indeed is my husband when, by asking my views on the coups, he assures me that my mind is still intact.

If I offer an opinion on the state of the world and my husband respectfully listens—and maybe agrees—I feel intellectually reassured. But if I launch into an animated account of the latest white sale, or my adventures at the hardware store, or why Mildred is divorcing Phil, and my husband *still* listens, I feel reassured that I am not (as I sometimes secretly fear) a witless bore.

I wish I could claim that I never discuss such dreary, trivial matters. But, like other wives, I often do. It's true I never *intended* to discuss them, and it's true that with the other men I know, I mostly discuss the Middle Eastern crisis. But each of us, in the privacy of our living room, with just the man we're married to to hear, also discusses the crisis in toilet training—and we want him to be listening when we do.

Not listening is probably the commonest unkindness of married life, and one that creates—more devastatingly than an eternity of forgotten birthdays and misguided Christmas gifts—an atmosphere of not loving and not caring. For if a husband tunes us out and doesn't hear us, if he doesn't want to know what's on our mind, he sets off a chilling logic that goes like this: He isn't interested, which means I'm not interesting, which means I'm unlovable, which means I'm unloved.

I heard about one desperate woman whose husband closed up his ears and sank into a television trance every night. Finally, in a dramatic bid for his attention, she announced that she had been knocked over by a bus, taken a lover, and withdrawn $2,000 from their joint checking account. Her husband didn't even blink. Then she marched over to him, grabbed his shoulder, and hollered, "Didn't you hear what I said? Listen to me, damn you!" To which her husband, without taking his eyes off the set, absently replied, "Yes, darling, of course I'm crazy about you."

Well, she simply doesn't believe him and I don't blame her. For women do not live by words alone. My husband lets me know that I am interesting by paying attention to the things I say, just as he informs me that I'm a good cook by finishing, in one sitting, the veal that I'd figured would last for two nights at least. And all the glib, rote phrases in the world would never compensate for his not hearing what I said, or for leaving the veal untouched.

I don't mean to imply that the loving word lacks the power to convey love. Of course it does, particularly when it is unsolicited, and even more particularly when it's uncalculated.

In other words, if I'm fresh from the hairdresser and dressed to the teeth and I plant myself in front of Milton and ask, "How do I look?" I stand an excellent chance of being told I look good. But how much nicer it is when he glances up as I'm giving final instructions to the sitter and volunteers a richly approving "Wow!"

Or take the evening of the big dinner party when the maid doesn't show up, and I clean every room in the house, smoothly get the children into bed, leap into my velvet hostess gown, and, poised and gracious, proceed to serve our ten guests a gorgeous Beef Wellington. If I remind my husband, after the guests go home, how hard it was, I'm certain he'll agree that yes, it sure was hard. And if I point out to him how well I think I did, he'll undoubtedly reassure me that yes, I sure did well. Ah, but what really knocks me out is when I don't have to tell him anything at all, when he—free of charge—says to me with genuine pride and delight, "You were fantastic."

There are other times, however, when words specifically left unsaid are a powerful way of making me feel cherished. Each of us occasionally earns for ourself a thoroughly justified "I told you so" from our husband. But when what Milton warned me would happen happens, and he nevertheless restrains himself from crowing about it, I cannot help but feel that love has triumphed over sanctimony. For silence is indeed golden when . . .

he said I should wash the towels by themselves, and I said the color definitely wouldn't run, and then the entire wash came out a horrible mottled green, and he said . . . nothing;

and when he said Nick looked sick, and I said since when did he have an M.D., and then the school sent Nick home with a fever of 105, and he said . . . nothing;

and when he said he smelled smoke, and I said he was always smelling something, and then we found a fire in the trash can because I had forgotten to stub out my cigarette, and he said . . . nothing.

Social situations are a whole other sensitive area where a husband's behavior, or misbehavior, conveys to us the presence or absence of love.

It's easy at cocktail parties to recognize the wife who feels unloved. She's been standing in the same corner for the past hour with an empty glass in her hand and no one to talk to, and her husband is busy researching every décolletage in the place and freshening up everyone's drink but hers. When she finally tracks him down and suggests they leave, he explains to everyone within earshot that she's a party pooper or having her period—and flatly refuses to go.

If she tells a story, he says that's not how it happened. If she tells a joke, he rushes in with the punch line. If she ventures an observation on the elections, he asks, loud and clear, how would she know, since she never reads the paper. And if she says again that they really have to get back because the sitter has a date at eight o'clock, he hands her the car keys and sends her home without him.

Most of the husbands I know, unlike that beast, do not embarrass their wives in public places. But my loving husband is more than merely polite. If I've just achieved some sweet success, he drops it smoothly into the conversation. If I tell a joke he listens—and he laughs. And whatever appreciation he shows for the décolletage of others, he makes it clear to the world that he likes mine too.

In public, and in private, I feel very deeply loved when my husband lets me know that he enjoys not only my cleavage but my company.

Some men seem to spend their entire marriage avoiding their wives—by disappearing behind their newspapers and working late at the office and running off to ball games with their buddies on weekends and always asking other couples to come along, whether it's for a night on the town or for two weeks at Cape Cod. And if a wife protests this arm's-length style of life and wonders aloud if he has any particular interest in *her*, the stock reply seems to be, "Well, I married you, didn't I?"

But "I married you" isn't good enough for me, or for any of the women that I know. For the loving husband shows us he's *glad* he married us—and maybe, on occasion, downright thrilled. He invites us to come to town and join him for lunch when there's nothing to celebrate. He invites us to come upstairs and join him in the shower when we've already taken one. And he lets us know that whatever he's planning to do will be better if he's doing it with us.

(Which is why I'm often watching the Washington Redskins, despite the fact that I'll never understand football. And why my husband often skis beginner slopes with me, despite the fact that he's an expert skier.)

How does a husband make a woman feel loved? All of us have our own special answers to give, though in some cases our initial response may be a grumbling, "Who *him?*" But after we've thought for a while, we can see how hundreds of inconsequential gestures, gestures that we have pretty much taken for granted, account for our good feelings about ourselves, our marriages, our lives.

My friend Cora told me she'd pondered this question while resentfully driving through rush-hour traffic to pick up her husband at work. The kids were busy fighting in the back, the windshield wipers weren't wiping too well, and why the hell couldn't he take the bus. And yet . . . And yet . . . By the time she'd finally got to his office, she said, she was so overcome by the niceness of her man that she flung the door open and threw herself into his arms.

I too, adding up almost 12 years of small lovingkindnesses, have been feeling quite mellow toward my own husband since I began considering this matter. I'm feeling so grateful, in fact, that I've decided just what I'm going to do on his next birthday.

It's morning, and when he awakes, I'll greet him with a tender kiss, a rhododendron for his study, and a bottle of his favorite after-shave lotion. Gazing fondly into his sleep-swollen eyes, I'll swear that he's even handsomer than he was on the day I married him. And then, when evening comes, and he's eating the pâté I made with my own two hands, and our three sons are singing—at my request—a medley of songs from a King Family Holiday Special, I'll lean forward and whisper, most sincerely, that I love him.